The Limits of Economic Science

Kluwer·Nijhoff Studies in Human Issues

Previously published books in the series:

The Limits of Economic Science

Essays on Methodology

Richard B. McKenzie

Professor of Economics, Clemson University

Senior Fellow, Heritage Foundation

Kluwer·Nijhoff Publishing
Boston   The Hague   London

Distributors for North America:

Kluwer·Nijhoff Publishing
Kluwer Boston, Inc.
190 Old Derby Street
Hingham, Massachusetts 02043, U.S.A.

Distributors outside North America:

Kluwer Academic Publishers Group
Distribution Centre
P.O. Box 322
3300AH Dordrecht, The Netherlands

Library of Congress Cataloging in Publication Data

McKenzie, Richard B.
  The limits of economic science.

  (Kluwer-Nijhoff studies in human issues)
  Bibliography: p.
  Includes index.
  1. Economics — Addresses, essays, lectures. 2. Economics —
Methodology — Addresses, essays, lectures.
I. Title. II. Series.
HB71.M39   1982   330   82-12680
ISBN   0-89838-116-9

Printed in the United States of America

To my daughter
Susan Elizabeth McKenzie

Contents

PREFACE

The essays in this volume were a challenge to me to write. I am an economist to the core, inclined to evaluate most observed behavior and public policies with conventional neoclassical theory. The essays represent my attempt to come to grips with the meaning and importance of what I try to do as a professional economist. They reflect my attempt to acquire a new and improved understanding of the usefulness and limitations of the writings of professional economists, especially my own. In this regard, although I hope others will find the thoughts useful, the volume represents a personal statement of how one economist views his and others' work. For that reason the discussion is often openly normative, tinged with the conviction that social discourse is more than costs and benefits and that economics cannot be fully evaluated by the methods — economic methods — that are the subject of the evaluation.

These essays could not have been written without considerable encouragement and help from colleagues and friends. The following people are recognized for having read one or more chapters and for having contributed critical, substantive comments: Diana Bailey, Wilfred Beckerman, Geoffrey Brennan, William Briet, James Buchanan, Delores Martin, David Maxwell, Mary Ann McKenzie, Warren Samuels, Robert Staaf, Richard Wagner, Karen Vaughn, and Bruce Yandle. I am very much in their debt. However, they should not be held accountable for any of the positions taken and any errors that may remain. Jill Williams and Betsy Gourlay deserve special thanks for typing the original manuscripts. Karen Lea Jones and Lisa Kiel did an outstanding job of computerizing the final draft of the book. Without their dedicated assistance this book would have been far more difficult to develop.

Several of the essays in this book appeared originally as journal articles: chapter 2 (*Journal of Economic Issues,* September 1978), chapter 3 (*Southern Economic Journal,* July 1979), chapter 4 (*Southern Economic Journal,* July 1980), chapter 5 (*Journal of Economic Issues,* September 1981), and chapter 7 (*Southern Economic Journal,* April 1981). Because of the importance of the work to the author and the extent to which it is cited, extensive excerpts of Frank Knight's "The Limitations of Scientific Method of Economics" is included in the appendix with permission of the Mrs. Ethel Knight. My articles are reprinted here with permission of the journals with only modest revisions, and the articles were adjusted for the purpose of making the arguments flow in a logical progression from chapter to chapter.

I am indebted to the J.R. Sirrine Foundation for partially funding the research that led to the development of these essays and this book.

Finally, every father should have a thirteen-year-old daughter like mine. She has been an inspiration to me and has contributed indirectly to all that I have written.

In spite of the foregoing, there is a science of economics, a true, and even exact, science, which reaches laws as universal as those of mathematics and mechanics. The greatest need for the development of economics as a growing body of thought and practice is an adequate appreciation of the meaning, and the limitations, of this body of accurate premises and rigorously established conclusions. It comes about in the same general way as all science, except in higher degree, i.e., through abstraction. There are no laws regarding the content *of economic behavior, but there are laws universally valid as to its* form. *There is an abstract rationale of all conduct which is rational at all, and a rationale of all social relations arising through the organization of rational activity. We cannot tell what particular goods any person will desire, but we can be sure that within limits he will prefer more of any good to less, and that there will be limits beyond which the opposite will be true. We do not know what specific things will be wealth at any given time, but we know quite well what must be the attitude of any sane individual toward wealth wherever a social situation exists which gives the concept meaning . . .*

> *Frank H. Knight*
> *"The Limitations of Scientific Method in Economics"*

1 INTRODUCTION

Books often have their origin in the most peculiar of circumstances. Knowing their origin can be helpful in understanding what the author has to say, a rule of thumb especially applicable to books in methodology. This particular book had its genesis in what may appear on the surface to be its antithesis, *The New World of Economics,* a text Gordon Tullock and I first published in 1975.[1] A word or two about the contents of that text and the professional reaction to it can be useful in putting the following essays in proper context. Such comments may explain why I became sufficiently interested in methodology to write on the subject and why, contrary to the admonition of some scholars, I believe studies in methodology are inherently important. I have become convinced that without an appreciation for the methodological issues in social science research, it can be difficult for us to comprehend exactly what we are communicating, as opposed to what we think we are saying, in our professional writings.

The New World of Economics

By surveying what economists have written on a wide variety of unconventional topics, *The New World* is, in part, an exploration into the fringes of economic research. The mere listing of topics covered seems to speak solely to the "unboundedness" of economic analysis: law, lying, cheating, presidential elections,

1

bureaucracy, human capital and learning theory, human sexual proclivities and exploitation, marriage, divorce, and the economic tendencies of rodents, termites, and the insane. *The New World* even includes a discussion of "child production," "why anything worth doing is not necessarily worth doing well," and the findings of sociobiologists. Following in the footsteps of Philip Wicksteed,[2] we discuss in every chapter the applicability of marginal analysis and utilize repeatedly basic economic concepts such as the downward sloping demand curve, diminishing returns, and cost.

The New World should be, as it has tended to be, judged more for its pedagogy — its capacity to interest beginning students in economics — than for its methodology. Its primary purpose has never been to break new ground in economic research, but rather to show students what economists are doing and to introduce students to the economic way of thinking as painlessly as possible and by way of varied reiteration.

Judging from the reviews and letters written to the publisher, *The New World* has been evaluated both positively and negatively for its seemingly open-ended methodology — as a statement of the power or, as the case may be, professional bankruptcy of much modern economic analysis.[3] Both the praise (that the array of topics covered reveals the universal applicability of economic axioms) and critical comments (reduced to the suggestion that such work tends to "frivolize" economic analysis) were expected but unsettling to both of us. Our view of the book has always stood in stark contrast to such extreme evaluations.[4]

Despite caveats concerning the limitations of the analysis in the preface and scattered throughout the chapters, the complimentary and critical comments *The New World* inspired caused me to question whether the message we intended was being garbled in its transmission, to wonder what was being read into our analysis that was not intended. We in no way intended to suggest that all behavior is "rational" or is amenable to economic analysis, as many seem to think (approvingly or disparagingly, as the case may be). The book's reception caused me to reflect formally, in print, on some rather basic questions that Professor Tullock and I could sidestep in *The New World:* if economic theory is, indeed, an "engine of analysis," a claim I readily support, does it not have *conceptual,* as opposed to *practical,* limitations in enhancing people's understanding of social relationships? If it does have conceptual limitations, as I have always presumed it does, what are they? Are its limitations, as some would suggest, solely practical in nature — that is, founded upon the trial-and-error efforts of individual researchers and on what seems to work in individual evaluative circumstances? Further and more fundamentally, can theory be evaluated properly and fully by practical considerations alone, by its predictive power, a position ardently supported by neoclassicists?

Such questions as these force us to probe even deeper: If economics can be used to "know" some things, but not everything, about social relationships, how do we "know" when the theory has reached its level of impotence in pushing back the frontiers of knowledge about *real-world* social relationships and has begun to be more accurately described as fanciful thinking about a world that exists only in mathematical and graphical form? If we economists do not understand the conceptual limitations of our work, "form" may be inadvertently substituted for "substance;" restated, understanding of our models will supplant understanding of social relationships. Where are the boundaries, and how do we know when they have been reached? These are the types of questions that must inevitably be addressed by economists who seek to expand the intellectual turf of their discipline and who really want to appreciate the nature of what they think they know.

The subject matter of economics, a *social* science, is intrinsically different from the subject matter of physics, a *physical* science, or so casual appraisal of the different disciplines indicates. The former presupposes subjective evaluations by, to some undefined extent, original and independent individuals. The latter is concerned with physical events that are inextricably tied by fixed relationships (or so it appears). The physical sciences are, relatively speaking, straightforward endeavors. They escape the murky intellectual problems associated with subjective evaluation by simply assuming they do not exist, a position that may eventually prove to be unsound (after all, rocks, mountains, and electrical currents may, as some physicists speculate, have a subjective capacity).[5] The straightforward application of *physical* scientific techniques to social concerns can lead to egregious errors. (Consider Einstein's use of his science in the analysis of social issues that bothered him, a topic in chapter 6.)

However, as argued more fully later, a theory devoid of subjective considerations can be an internally consistent, predictive science in the sense and to the extent that objective, observable real-world events can be used to confirm the validity of predictions. In other words, a clear and unambiguous correspondence between theoretical variables and real-world empirical proxies is possible. The presumed fixity of physical relationships also permits predictions of specific events, as opposed to "patterns" of outcomes. Any inaccuracy in predictions can be attributed, as is done, to a lack of theory — meaning, a lack of understanding of fundamental laws (as in the case of laws that govern the movements of electrons around the nucleus of the atom) — and not to a lack of "constants" (or measurables) or to more or less spontaneous changes in subjective evaluations.

To the extent that a theory presumes a subjective capacity on the part of individual actors who are central elements in the theory, we must wonder in what sense economic science can be predictive and can emulate the methodological approach of physical science. This means we must question the extent to which subjectivity must be denied when *precise* predictive ability is sought. We must wonder, in short, if basic axioms regarding human nature do not bind, as Frank Knight suggested,[6] the predictive capacity and usefulness of economics. These are some of the questions partially explored in the following chapters.

Chapter 2 is, for the most part, a historical survey of the methodological views of three economists: Philip Wicksteed, Frank Knight, and Friedrich Hayek, who prominently evaluated in their writings the limits of economics. Methodological distinctions are drawn among three types of thinking processes: a "logic of choice," an "abstract science," and a "predictive science." Nonrational behavior is discussed in detail in chapter 3. The chapter addresses directly the issue of whether all human behavior can be construed conceptually as "rational" and discusses the limitations the "nonrational domain" of behavior imposes on economic science.

Chapter 4 deals with the issue of whether economic science can be strictly nonnormative, and chapter 5 compares and attempts a partial reconciliation of two schools of modern economic thought, the Austrian and neoclassical schools. Chapter 6 considers somewhat indirectly the methodological compatibility of physical science and economics by surveying the economics of Albert Einstein and by explaining how Einstein's physics influenced (and misdirected) his economic commentary.

On Defining Boundaries of Science

The problem of establishing the limits of economic science is neither trivial nor easy to resolve. Defining the discipline's boundaries is important because of the growing reliance public policymakers place on "economic science" in developing government programs for a wide range of perceived social concerns, from parenting to caring for the elderly. Establishing the boundaries of economics would be simple if economics were devoid of useful insights; however, the contrary is surely the case, even when economists have imperialistically rummaged through the traditional domains of other disciplines. The concepts of the downward sloping demand curve and opportunity costs are powerful predictive tools when compared with the central theoretical concepts of other disciplines like sociology. Because of the work of economists, many people now understand more firmly than ever that trades freely negotiated are mutually beneficial and that many public policy obstructions to trade destroy its potential to promote mutual gains and, thereby, cause misallocation of resources. The public can now appreciate, because of the professional insistence of economists, that inflation and growth in the money stock are inextricably bound through the equation of exchange. Additionally, when economists have stepped outside the strict confines of monetary and trading relationships, insights have been offered in response to a number of social questions, some important, some not so important.

Why Are More Women Working Now Than in the Past? Other social sciences point to changes in "inculturated social values," to an "awakening" of women to their own individuality and productive capacity, while economists stress the role of the mechanization of housework and the growth in the wage rates of women. Social values may have changed, but such changes do not nullify the complementary economic explanation.

Why Has There Been a Growth in the Restaurant Business? Economists, once again, point to the impact of rising wage rates on the cost of "home-produced meals" and of rising incomes on the demand for fully prepared meals. Again, such explanations tend to be overlooked by other social scientists.

Why Has the Birthrate Declined? The typical economist's refrain is that children are expensive "goods" that have become relatively more expensive over recent decades. Children are labor-intensive, and the "price" of children has increased along with the rise in the opportunity cost of parenting. Concomitantly, the prices of many other nonhuman goods and services, which are relatively less labor-intensive, have fallen with advancements in technology. The disparity in the growth in productivity of producing children and in nonhuman goods and services has resulted in a marginal shift from children to nonhuman goods and services.

Why Do Students Fail to Learn Economics? The typical answer is that the teachers are unqualified or the subject matter, too hard or the books and learning aids, substandard. Economists may explain, however, that because economics course work is designed to upgrade the political intelligence of the citizenry, economic education is, to a considerable extent, a public good. Students, like the proverbial fisherman contemplating the construction of a lighthouse, quite rationally avoid the production of public goods at their own expense.

These statements are not necessarily the most profound economists have to offer about the human predicament, but anyone wishing to question the presumption that economics is unbounded must grant that such lines of analysis do contribute "something" to continuing policy debates. For example, economic analysis of fertility suggests that population growth is, at least in part, a self-correction process; and consideration of the economic incentives (or, rather the lack of them) goes a long way toward explaining why many people are ill-informed about the issues involved in most elections and fail to vote.

Having appropriately applauded such contributions, we must still wonder if blind, unquestioning extensions of economic analysis are, at some point, counterproductive. As I argue in considerable detail in the following chapters, the limitations of economic science relate principally to the nature of the assumptions underlying economic models and the purposes of economic theory.

With their successes close at hand, it is all too easy for economists to slide smoothly from the *correct* methodological position that assumptions of rational behavior and profit maximization can be used for making empirically refutable, if only tentative, predictions to the *incorrect* methodological presumption that all behavior is rational and/or that all firms strictly profit-maximize. In short, it is very easy for the researcher to assume that the theoretical, and admittedly sterile and unreal, assumptions undergirding economic models (and not the predictions relating to observable outcomes) are the object of empirical refutation — that predictive assumptions are, when subjected to repeated successful tests, mental constructs for descriptive reality. George Stigler seems to have made the transition just suggested with considerable ease in his Tanner Lectures at Harvard University:

> Do people possess ethical beliefs which influence their behavior in ways not dictated by, and hence in conflict with, their own long-run utility-maximizing behavior? . . . This question of the existence of effective ethical values is, of course, an empirical question and in principle should be directly testable . . . Let me predict the outcome of the systematic and comprehensive testing of behavior in situations where self-interest and ethical values with wide verbal allegiance are in conflict. Much of the time, most of the time in fact, the self-interest theory . . . will win . . . I predict this result because it is the prevalent result found by economists not only within a wide range of economic phenomena, but in the investigations of marital, child-bearing, criminal, religious and other social behavior. We believe that man is a utility-maximizing animal . . . and to date we have not found it informative to carve out a section of life in which he invokes a different goal behavior.[7]

And Stigler adds at the close of his lecture:

> I arrive at . . . the thesis that flows naturally and irresistably from the theory of economics. Man is eternally a utility-maximizer — in his home, in his office (be it public or private), in his church, in his scientific work — in short, everywhere. He can and often does err: perhaps because the calculation is too difficult. He learns to correct those errors, although sometimes at heavy cost. What we call ethics, on this approach, is a set of rules with respect to dealings with other persons, rules which in general prohibit behavior which is only myopically self-serving, or which imposes large costs on others with small gains to oneself. General observance of these rules makes not only for long-term gains to the actor but also yields outside benefits, and the social approval of the ethics is a mild form of enforcement of the rules to achieve this general benefit.[8]

Clearly, many other professional economists, like Stigler, confuse *homo economicus* (a theoretical device) with real-world human beings. They seem to acknowledge that if people are not exactly like *homo economicus,* the difference between what they are like and are assumed to be like in economic models is of no great consequence. Clarifying prospective confusions between predictive assumptions and descriptive reality is as important to studies in methodology as clarifying the distinction between movements along and shifts in demand is to basic economics courses. More, however, is required to make the argument enduring than the presentation of counter examples; instances in which people obviously do not behave rationally or in a self-serving (or self-interested) manner are not sufficient proof of the restrictiveness of economic models to economists like Stigler. Such "proofs" can be cast aside when predictions are set in probabilistic terms. More needs to be said about the internal consistency of the assumptions with the predictive intent of the theory (a main focus of these chapters).

Without an appreciation for methodological issues in much modern economic research, it is quite easy for a researcher to assume that models give not only some "understanding" of social events (in the limited sense that variables are mentally organized and linked by way of mathematical formulas), but also yield to the researcher significant power (or more power than would exist in the absence of tested theory) over future human events. Clearly, scientific procedures have a twofold function: to provide understanding and to permit control — that is, to alter future outcomes. Understanding does not necessarily imply control (or even the desire to control). Indeed, as Chicago economists have shown, economic theory can be used to show the futility and counterproductive nature of many modern control efforts. However, researchers who fail to see the limited authority of their theories may assume greater arrogance than is warranted concerning their capacity to control human behavior by way of government policies. Methodological studies tend to shore up professional humility by exposing the narrowness of some conclusions (including policy implications).

Purposes as Limitations on Theory

Contrary to the persistent claims of strict neoclassicists, theoretical inquiries are not directed solely at one monolithic goal: prediction as established by empirical tests. And it should come as no surprise that the purposes that guide the construction of theory play a role in determining the limitations of the theory. Some theoretical work is directed simply at organizing the "great buzzing confusions of information" that we confront on a daily basis. The assumptions we make and "logic" we employ are satisfactory to the extent that they accomplish that goal, or enable us to "make sense" of what we observe passing by our narrow window on the physical or social universe. In this regard, predictions play a secondary role, if they play a role at all, in the scientific process. This type of theory may be an expression of a very precise tautological statement, like the equation of exchange, or the "logic of choice," or the identity between aggregate income and expenditures. Such statements are useful, nonetheless, since they provide a system of classifying real-world events.

On the other hand, theory can be designed to make predictions, but such a purpose imposes its own restrictions on what can be logically deduced and empirically confirmed. In addition, predictions differ in the specificity of expected outcomes. As discussed in chapter 4, neoclassicists and Austrians disagree, partially because they have different theoretical purposes and interests. Neoclassicists seek to develop a means by which very specific social consequences can be predicted within an already adopted constitutional framework; neoclassical economics requires a very precise form of rationality (captured in the specificity of the goods in individuals' utility functions) to undergird its theory. Neoclassical studies are decidedly "postconstitution" and policy directed.

Austrians wish to devise a means of predicting the kinds of "patterns of outcomes" and explaining the processes through which those patterns are likely to emerge. Austrian "rationality" can be captured in the very general notion that people either know, or will learn within tolerable limits, what is best for them and will seek to improve their positions in life, with no mention of what it is that is pursued. Empirically refutable predictions are irrelevant to Austrians because they are not sought; the only prediction made refers to the "orderliness" (in the case of a "constitution of liberty") of the emerging patterns of relationships among individuals, something not readily refutable by empirical tests.

Geoffery Brennan and James Buchanan have very recently reasserted what they believe is *the* long-standing purpose of theoretical assumption, such as rational behavior, in political economy.[9] They argue rather convincingly that early political economists such as Adam Smith were primarily constitutionalists. That is, they were mainly interested in searching out the necessary constraints on government that would protect people from fully rational, self-seeking individuals who might use government to further their own interests at the expense of everyone else. From this perspective, rational, self-seeking behavior is the "worst case" (not the predictive case or the descriptive case) from which people will naturally seek to protect themselves by way of constitutional limits on what government can do.

In seeking to have a house built (an example employed by Brennan and Buchanan), people may choose their builder on the basis of recognized professional integrity and desire to do the job right. But in constructing a mutually binding contract they will be inclined to assume the worst — that the builder is totally self-centered and self-seeking — because that is the type of person they seek to protect themselves against. Such a methodological position is suitable for Brennan and Buchanan, for much of their analysis is explicitly normative. It seeks "appropriate institutional design:"

> The question we are interested in posing about any particular social order is whether the rules by which individual actions are coordinated are such as to transform actions undertaken by participants in their own *private* interests into outcomes that are in the interests of others. We know that this curious alchemy is in fact worked by the *market* — that the invisible hand operates, under certain more or less well-defined conditions, to convert private interest into public interest. The prime task of comparative institutional analysis is to inquire whether other institutions do the same, and, if so, whether those institutions do so under more or less restrictive conditions . . .

In constitutional design, and in comparative institutional analysis more generally, one's particular beliefs about what model of man is empirically most descriptive are less relevant in precisely the same way and for much the same reason. One calls forth the *homo economicus* assumption, not because it is necessarily the most accurate model of human behavior but because it is the appropriate model for testing whether institutions serve to transform private interest into public. It is as simple as that.[10]

Brennan and Buchanan add:

For the purposes of predictive science, the elements in individual utility functions must be specified in clear, recognizable and measurable terms. Application of the *homo economicus* construction for empirical or predictive purposes requires something like the assumption of net wealth maximization as a surrogate for maximization of consumption more broadly achieved. For constitutional design, however, *homo economicus* can be seen to maximize almost anything at all, providing each individual conceives of others as operating without *his* interests in mind . . . *This* version of the *homo economicus* model in no sense rules out the possibility that each individual may be motivated by certain ethical or moral concerns, as long as we can take it that such ethical conduct on the part of anyone cannot be presumed to benefit everyone else.[11]

Concluding Comments

The following chapters expand upon what has been said here. Theory is not unlike instruments, which are designed to meet the specific needs of the practitioner; and therein lies the basis for the tools' limitations. The same can be said about mental, economic tools of analysis. No one should be surprised to learn they also have their limitations. Sorting out those limitations is not easy, and explaining them will tax our capacity to communicate.

Notes

1. Richard B. McKenzie and Gordon Tullock, *The New World of Economics: Explorations into Human Behavior* (Homewood, Ill.: Richard D. Irwin, 1975, 1978, and 1981).

2. Philip H. Wicksteed, *The Common Sense of Political Economy* (New York: Augustus M. Kelly, 1967).

3. For contrasting reviews of *The New World*, see Lawrence H. Officer and Leanna Stiefel, "The New World of Economics: A Review Article," *Journal of Economic Issues*, March 1976, pp. 149–58; Charles P. Fishbaugh, book review section, *Review of Business and Economics*, Winter 1976, pp. 90–93; and *Wall Street Journal*, January 25, 1981, editorial page.

4. We wrote in the preface the following:

By using tools of economic analysis as we have (admittedly, in some cases, in an exploratory and venturesome manner), there is the ever-present possibility for misunderstanding. *Economic method does not cover all phases of human life. Hence, when economics is applied to new areas, it does not give a complete picture* . . . [I]n many of these areas we discuss in this book, our approach is partial, rather than complete, modeling of the world . . . Nevertheless, we think that these economic models are enlightening even if they do not give complete answers. [emphasis added, *The New World of Economics,* 1981, p. x]

5.   See David Zukav, *The Dancing of the Wu Li Masters* (New York: Bantum Books, 1980).

6.   Frank H. Knight, "The Limitations of Scientific Method in Economics," *The Ethics of Competition* (Chicago: University of Chicago Press, 1976), pp. 105–47.

7.   George Stigler, *Lecture II,* Tanner Lectures delivered at Harvard University, April 1980, pp. 23–24.

8.   George Stigler, *Lecture III,* Tanner Lectures delivered at Harvard University, April 1980, as quoted in Geoffrey Brennan and James Buchanan, "The Normative Purpose of Economic 'Science': Rediscovery of an Eighteenth Century Method," *International Review of Law and Economics* (Winter 1981), p. 158.

9.   Brennan and Buchanan, "The Normative Purpose."

10.   Ibid., pp. 160–161.

11.   Ibid., pp. 161–162.

2 ON THE METHODOLOGICAL BOUNDARIES OF ECONOMIC ANALYSIS:
A Review and Partial Synthesis

Jacob Viner once defined *economics* as what economists do. With this rather imprecise definition of the discipline, the most casual reader of journals may conclude that economists "do" a lot more than they once did, that the permissible boundaries of economic investigation are conceived by a sizable segment of the profession as being much broader than they once were. Although we may rightly differ over the worthiness of the topics that have been investigated, it is difficult to deny the growth in the diversity of studies undertaken in the past two decades.

There is now a significant body of literature on the economics of crime, fertility, family relations, discrimination, anarchy, political decisionmaking, charity, human capital of all forms, constitutional development, ethics, law, bureaucratic management, and (to a limited extent) sexual behavior. The scholarly work being done in these "new" areas is epitomized by the work of Gary Becker.[1] His views are briefly summarized by this resolute statement:

> Indeed I have come to the conclusion that the economic approach is a comprehensive one that is applicable to *all* human behavior, be it behavior involving money prices or imputed shadow prices, repeated or infrequent decisions, large or minor decisions, emotional or mechanical ends, rich or poor persons, adults or children, brilliant or stupid persons, patients or therapists, businessmen or politicians, teachers or students.[2]

This is a revised version of an article that appeared in the September 1978 issue of the *Journal of Economic Issues*. Reprinted by special permission of the copyright holder, the Association for Evolutionary Economics.

11

In addition, elements of conventional economic analysis undergird the philosophical work of John Rawls,[3] the sociological exchange theory of Anthony Heath,[4] and the experimental work in the economic-psychology of John Kagel, Vernon Smith, Charles Plott, and Ray Batallio.[5] As noted in chapter 1, *The New World of Economics* provides beginning students with an introduction to a number of these research areas.[6]

In line with the continuing expansion of economic analysis into new and untested areas, skepticism is increasing about the usefulness of economic analysis in many areas.[7] Indeed, among a relatively small group of economists evidence of hostility is growing toward the extension of economics into every nook and cranny of behavior. However, the voices of the critics serve the important purpose of raising a question that is all too easily ignored by those of us who are, perhaps, too enthusiastically "pushing back the frontiers" and attempting to test the elasticity of economic methodology: If we reject Becker's view and accept the position that economics cannot explain all human experience, then how far *can* or even *should* we stretch the application of our basic models? Phrased in more concrete terms, if economic analysis can be applied to political decisionmaking, as Lawrence Officer and Leanna Stiefel seem to agree that it can be,[8] can it not be applied to marriage and to sexual behavior, as they seem to think it cannot?[9] What are the limitations of the methods we use? Where do we draw the line or, to pose the question in other terms, is Becker's position a logical and reasonable extension of traditional economic analysis?

The purpose of this chapter is to address these questions and to consider, somewhat indirectly the criticisms of the skeptics, not as they specifically apply to my own work in *The New World*, but as they apply to the trend of economic analysis. I seek to accomplish these ends by reviewing and synthesizing here the thoughts of three of the handful of economists who have made clarification of the boundaries of economic analysis part and parcel of their broader work. They are Philip Wicksteed, Frank Knight, and Friedrich Hayek. Their views are important, not only because they are prominent authors, but also because they are, in some respects, the intellectual predecessors of economists, such as Becker, who have extended the application of economic methods. The boundaries of economic analysis are not drawn with precision in the works of these authors; however, their arguments eliminate some of the fuzziness with which the boundaries are presently perceived and illuminate some of the issues at stake in defining those boundaries.

The Logic of Choice and Its Boundaries

While W.S. Jevons is remembered for formulating precisely the equimarginal rule for consumer utility maximization, Philip Wicksteed is recognized for having extended its application to almost everything people value, and the critics are correct in suggesting that such contemporary economic discussions are not new. Indeed, a repeated theme of Wicksteed's classic *The Common Sense of Political Economy* is: "It follows that the general principles which regulate our conduct in business are identical with those which regulate our deliberations, our selections between alternatives, and our decisions, in all branches of life. And this is why we may not only, but must take our ordinary experiences as the starting point for approaching economic problems."[10] Later, he writes: "If political economy has any laws of its own, we have yet to discover them."[11] This statement resembles Becker's position summarized in the statement above (and George Stigler's position enunciated in chapter 1).

To Wicksteed, the equimarginal rule provided, as it does to contemporary economists, the basis for a logic of how people behave with regard to those things they value, whether they are embodied in conventional or nonconventional "goods:" "When we are considering whether we will live in the country or the town, we may find, on examination, that we are carefully equating increments and decrements of such apparently heterogeneous indulgences as those associated with fresh eggs and friendship. Or, more generally, the inner core of our life problems and the gratification of all our ultimate desires . . . obey the same allpermeating law."[12] The heterogeneous indulgences that Wicksteed cites at various points in his book include virtue, wisdom, sagacity, prudence, honor, success, literature, sex, art, education, and spiritual enjoyment. Several passages clearly reveal his perception of the diversity of human behavior to which the equimarginal rule can be applied:

Shall I "bury myself in the country," where I shall see little of my dearest friends, but may hope for fresh eggs for breakfast and fresh air all the day? Or shall I stay where I am, and continue to enjoy the society of my friends?[13]

An ardent lover may decline a business interview in order to keep an appointment with his lady-love, but there will be some point at which its estimated bearing upon his prospects of an early settlement will make him break his appointment with the lady in favor of the business interview.[14]

Whether our housewife is apportioning the stuffing of a goose at the table, or her housekeeping money in the market, or her time and attention between schemes for getting or keeping a connection for boarders and the more direct cultivation and furthering of the general tastes and interests of her life; and whether her husband is conducting family prayers, or posting up his books at the office, or weighing the advantages and disadvantages of a partial retirement from business; whether, in a word, either or both of them are pursuing their ultimate purpose in life and obeying their fundamental impulses by direct or indirect means, they and all the people they are concerned with are alike engaged in administering resources, in developing opportunities and choosing between alternatives, under the great controlling guidance of the two principles we have been continuously illustrating throughout our investigations.[15]

In effect, Wicksteed postulates a completely open-ended utility function, which, by its nature, implies that only the individual knows what will be maximized or over what range of "goods" the equimarginal rule applies. Today, many scholars, including Becker, start with the same conception of human nature. Armen Alchian and William Allen follow Wicksteed very closely. They write that the individual values many different goods and goals and cite a list of examples that could have come straight out of *Common Sense*: "prestige, power, other people's welfare, love, respect, self-expression, talent, liberty, knowledge, beauty, leisure."[16] Other contemporary writers have simply modified Wicksteed's analysis by introducing additional nontraditional "goods" into the individual's utility function. Economists who have studied political decisionmaking have added the vote as one of a number of goods politicians are assumed to maximize; economists who have studied fertility have added children, or to use their more precise terminology, "child services." Similarly, those who study crime have assumed that the criminal views crime or criminal behavior as a good or, perhaps, more accurately, as a legitimate means of achieving other ends that are left unspecified. Those who have written about government bureaucracy have postulated that bureaucrats maximize their budgets, and students of the "new home economics" have assumed that family members individually and/or collectively maximize "home-produced goods."

All of this "new" research seems to be a straightforward, logical extension of Wicksteedian economics: The individual is assumed to have wants, which can be anything, and regardless of what those wants are, the individual will follow the equimarginal rule. By identifying the good or goods in the individual's utility function, the equilibrium conditions can be specified; external, institutional changes, similar to changes in relative prices or incomes, can be postulated; and predictions can be made as to how the utility maximizing individual will respond. However, similarity between the work of Wicksteed as we have defined it here and the current studies of scholars in Becker's mold is illusory.

Wicksteed's foremost interest was in articulating a logic of choice, as distinguished from, to use James Buchanan's classification, an *abstract science* of the Knightian tradition or of a *predictive science* of the contemporary Chicago school, into which Becker's work falls.[17] In concentrating on formulating a logic of choice, Wicksteed was uninterested (at least at the beginning of his book) in specifying exactly what is in the individual's utility function. The utility function is indeed open-ended, determined subjectively, all of which leaves ample room for a creative consciousness, which, within limits, imposes itself on the external world and does not merely respond to it. The many examples Wicksteed uses, although reasonable first approximations, are merely illustrations of what *can be* in the utility function, not what *is*. They are a means of suggesting to the reader the nature and plausibility of his a priori statements.

The equimarginal rule follows logically from the implied assumption that people act purposefully a significant portion of the time.[18] The Wicksteedian formulation of choice behavior is fully explanatory of all *purposeful* behavior in the conventional sense of the term, which is another way of saying that it is empty of specific predictive content. It is, as a logic of choice, a mode of thought and is satisfactory only to the extent that it organizes thinking about how people behave in general; and the logic of choice outlines, to use Hayek's terminology, the broad abstract properties of behavior, but says nothing about the specific concrete content of behavior.[19]

The message of the preceding paragraphs is reasonably clear: With an open-ended utility function, one cannot move to predictions of what people will actually do, given changes in circumstances. All such predictions require that a "good," such as "child services," be specified objectively in order that one can determine that the prediction has been confirmed or refuted by experience; but there can be no objective statement of what a "good" is at the logic-of-choice level of abstraction. To specify goods objectively would, furthermore, be contrary to the theoretical intent of the logic-of-choice paradigm, which is simply to present the broad outlines of behavior in order that the broad outlines of social organization may be discussed, as Hayek has attempted to do in his most recent three-volume work.[20]

"Child services," for example, means different things to different people. Whatever it means, we should expect people to follow the equimarginal rule with regard to child services as they, individually, define the good. However, there is no reason why we should expect people, who perceive child services in different ways, to respond in an objective, predictable manner when institutional changes occur. This is because the good is simply not specified, and there is no way of determining — that is, of objectively predicting — the relationship between institutional changes and some unknown, in the sense that it is unidentified, good.

A central point of divergence between Becker and Wicksteed now becomes apparent. To Becker, who is squarely in the positive tradition, Chicago style, the only meaningful statements are those with predictive content in the sense that they are empirically refutable. This is the essential message of Milton Friedman's seminal methodological essay.[21] Empirical refutation requires that the good be objectively specified, which totally conflicts with Wicksteed's open-ended utility function. The logic of choice and Becker's predictive science are, therefore, two conceptually distinct methodological paradigms. In other words, there is a methodological jump in moving from a logic of choice to a predictive science, a jump that seems to have gone largely unrecognized by many economists involved in "pushing back the frontiers." In the Wicksteedian formulation, a good is that which corresponds to a downward sloping demand curve, derived ex post to behavior. The two concepts of demand and good are inseparable, conceptually the same, as Buchanan has noted in reference to the open-ended utility function of

Alchian and Allen.[22] In the positive tradition of Becker, the objectivity of the good is identified independently of any observed behavior, and it is this independent identification that makes room for predictions of how people will behave, for example, when the price falls. A simple market transaction, a form of observed behavior, does not, as Buchanan has noted, define a good: The persons in the market can exchange bads.[23] That is, they can give up something more disliked than that good received. Hence, prediction requires that the definitions of the good and of behavior be conceptually separated. To Wicksteed, or in the context of any logic of choice, the good is a good because people are observed to buy less of it when the price is raised. The law of demand at this level of analysis is a description of behavior, not a predictive tool; nor is it intended to be one.

It should be stressed that when Wicksteed develops the open-ended utility function, he is not concerned with developing a model of behavior with specific predictive content.[24] Rather, his purpose is to explain how people behave and the emergence of what he calls "exchange relationships," which are, in his view, the restricted domain of political economy. He is not interested in predicting exactly what will emerge, in the sense of saying what people will buy or produce themselves, but rather in explaining the "economic harmonies" of what does in fact emerge:

> When we see the world, in virtue of its millions of mutual adjustments, carrying itself on from day to day, and ask "Who sees to it all?" and receive no answer, we can well understand the religious awe and enthusiasm with which an earlier generation of economists contemplated those "economic harmonies," in virtue of each individual, in serving himself, of necessity serves his neighbor, and by simply obeying the pressures about him, following the path that opens before him, weaves himself into the pattern of "purposes he cannot measure."[25]

A semblance of prediction, albeit implicit, exists here. There is, in the logic of choice, a prediction of what Hayek has called "patterns of outcomes."[26] The predicted pattern is the economic harmony, but the prediction is conceptually different from that embodied in any statement of what people will in fact do with regard to a specific good and specific changes in market conditions. Similar to Charles Darwin's theory of evolution, as Hayek notes, the logic of choice is distinguished more for the types of unexpected patterns of behavior than for the expected patterns. According to Hayek, its usefulness emanates from its presumption of our unalterable ignorance of human behavior; it thereby forces us to think, not in terms of predicting and controlling the "content" of people's behavior, but in terms of seeking out "abstract rules" of social organization within which a "spontaneous order" can emerge and the content of people's behavior can be *freely* determined. "Rules are a device for coping with our constitutional ignorance. There would be no need for rules among omniscient people who were in agreement on the relative importance of all the different ends. Any examination of the moral or legal order which leaves this fact out of account misses the central problem."[27]

Obviously, the logic of choice, including deductions about how exchanges and the spontaneous order arise, represents to Hayek the methodological boundaries of economic analysis. He is interested in formulating just rules of conduct, which, as he argues in a Rawlsian sense, can only be agreed upon in a state of ignorance of specific future outcomes. Accordingly, the logic of choice is the methodological equivalent of the Rawlsian veil of ignorance, which cannot and, for that matter, should not be transgressed in discussing social questions. Any predictive science in the Becker sense can only lead to control, an authoritarian state, and to the moral debasement of the rules of social organization — if it serves any purpose at all, which Hayek and Knight seriously doubt.[28] Once people know the outcome or the concrete content of social organization, they have reason to distort the rules to suit their own interests. Whether the rules are just can then be disputed openly. Restricting social inquiry is, therefore, to Hayek and other Austrian economists a moral imperative. This may explain why Austrians attack much modern neoclassical economics with such religious fervor (a subject extensively treated in chapter 4). In addition, from the point of view of Hayek and Knight, predicting specific outcomes is virtually impossible. Hayek denounces such attempts as "scientism," which leads to the wasting of intellectual energies in a futile debate over the meaning of "social or distributive justice" of outcomes, as distinguished from the justice of rules of social organization.

A semblance of predictive content emerges because even the logic of choice postulates purposeful behavior, as separated from all other forms of behavior that can conceivably be postulated. If all conceivable forms of behavior are postulated as a part of the analytical starting point, then nothing can be said of significance. There will, in fact, be no explanation of anything because explanations, by their nature, necessitate theoretical restrictions on how people are expected to behave. It is at this juncture that Hayek and Knight, and in particular the latter, question how much of human experience economic analysis as a logic of choice can explain. Knight writes:

> The problem of life is to utilize resources "economically," to make them go as far as possible in the production of desired results. The general theory of economics is therefore simply the rationale of life. — In so far as it has any rationale. The first question in regard to scientific economics is this question of how far life is rational, how far its problems reduce to the form of using given means to achieve given ends. Now this, we shall contend, is not very far.[29]

Knight goes on to argue that "life is at bottom an exploration of the field of values, an attempt to discover values, rather than on the basis of knowledge of them to produce and enjoy them to the greatest possible extent."[30]

In short, although economic analysis illuminates a certain dimension of human experience, Knight would surely dispute Becker's claim that the economic approach is applicable to *all* human behavior. Becker and those who accept his methodological framework may argue that the economic approach — the logic of choice — is still applicable at the level at which we seek to determine what we value. This position seems to be intrinsic to the study of the "economics of information." We do have choices to make over the kind and amount of information, including information on our own values, we will acquire. At one level, there is an optimizing problem; however, the analysis cannot be extended very far without confronting an infinite regress that forms another methodological limit to analysis: If we use resources in an economic way to determine what we value, then how do we go about using our resources to determine in an economic way how we go about using our resources to determine what we value, and so on, ad infinitum? At some point, individuals must assert in some noncalculating way how they will use resources to establish what they want: They must, in effect, take a stab in the dark, which perhaps cannot be explained in any more satisfactory way than to say that it is done. Recognizing the problem of the infinite regress and the ultimate nonrational base for establishing preferences, it is no wonder that economists typically begin their analysis with *given* individual values and say little about how those values change. To do otherwise is to run headlong into Knight's implied question: How much of human experience is rational?

Unfortunately, I know of no way of settling the question short of empirical testing, to which Knight would object because the concepts at stake are not subject to measurement. If only a small portion of the human experience is guided by purposeful, rational behavior in the conventional sense, then Knight has a reasonable objection to extending economic analysis to the point that it relies, for its validity, on the degree to which its predictions are confirmed by measured evidence. An economic prediction at the conceptual level can be quite correct; however, the evidence may never show this to be true since the rational component of behavior is continually overwhelmed by the nonrational components. Furthermore, Knight was very Austrian in the sense that he worried about the looseness of the connection between what people actually choose and empirical measures of their choices. When we put something in an individual's utility function, we usually identify its physical properties, such as those of apples. However, when people make choices they do not choose some good like apples with homogeneous properties; rather, they choose "images" of apples, which vary from person to person. At times the correspondence between the measured "responses" of people and the actual "choices" that people make may be quite high; however, at other times, the correspondence may be very poor. In these latter cases, the underlying theory may be quite sound, but the empirical work may not show this. For these reasons, Knight insists that economic analysis must remain an "abstract science of behavior" whose arguments are not conceptually refutable. On the other hand, it is understandable that economists who adhere firmly to the strict positive tradition, as does Becker, also take the view that most, if not all, behavior is rational and concentrate on the objective similarity of goods.

From a Logic of Choice to a Predictive Science

There is a subtle but important methodological jump from assuming purposeful behavior, which is the kind of behavioral restriction necessary to say anything, to assuming what goes into an individual's utility function. This jump is the one economists working in many of the new areas have made. For good reasons, this methodological jump has its detractors as well as supporters, even among those who understand what the jump is all about. An assumption of purposeful behavior is a very broad assertion about how people, in general, behave. Because of its very generality, its nonspecificity, it finds broad, although not universal, acceptance. Furthermore, the pattern of behavior that is predicted is similarly general, so much so that the analysis makes no suggestion as to how an individual's behavior should be controlled or, accordingly, modified. That which emerges, emerges — that is that.[31]

On the other hand, economists such as Becker who specify the various goods in the individual's utility function are likely to meet with almost instant opposition from some quarters, especially if the good to be maximized is specified as something like "children" or "child services." Disagreement will be extensive over what constitutes children or child services, over the significance of the specified service within an individual's utility function, and over what will be done with any finding. Specifying the components of the individual's utility function forces us to turn our interest away from understanding the patterns of behavior toward making more specific predictions about what people will actually do. To accomplish this end, we must not only introduce some goods to the individual's utility function, but take away others.

The nature of a predictive science, incorporating empirical verification, requires that individuals maximize, for example, the *quantity* of children. Individuals cannot, as a matter of objective science, maximize what they consider to be, for example, "soft-spoken children." The dictates of measurement, which define meaningful statements in Becker's methodology, and of mathematical manipulation become operational constraints on individuals' utility functions and on economic analysis. At some point in predictive science there must be a denial of the complete subjectivity of goods. Therefore, the analysis moves away from any pretense of dealing with purposeful behavior, in the sense that a creative consciousness controls behavior and looks to all of those external, environmental factors that define the "objectivity" of the good. As opposed to being studied as it is, the human experience is "molded" to fit the dictates of science, not the other way around. Critics rightfully question whether science has stepped over another methodological boundary and is no longer doing what was intended to be done. They maintain that the constraints of the process of science prohibit it from dealing with *all* human behavior.

Knight suggests that science gives emphasis to those dimensions of the human experience that are subject to manipulation or control. He writes: "The immediate purpose of science is to enable us to *understand,* which again covers the understanding both of beauty and of the technique of action. But our modern, sophisticated way of thinking tends more and more to subordinate the desire for understanding as such to a desire for control . . . A scientific age tends to relegate understanding for its own sake to the realm of sentiment and romance, an order of value regarded rather contemptuously in comparison with considerations of practice and power."[32] Whereas Knight argues that the complexity of human experience is so great that scientific methods can hardly improve upon what we can deduce from common sense, Hayek stresses, in addition, that attempts at control raise the specter of social or distributive justice, which, as we have noted, is meaningless to him.[33] In summary, control can lead only to governmental "intrusion" into the spontaneous order and to a disruption of it.

From a Predictive Science to Control

Why do economists care about the policy implications of their models? The answer must, in some way, be that we believe something is wrong with a state that emerges from the completely free and voluntary interaction of people. Any criterion derived externally from the emerging market process must force us, as it did Wicksteed, to move from the generality of the logic of choice to a predictive science. After talking about the role of ethics in human experience and of the market as a means to an end, Wicksteed states: "But the more we analyze the life of society, the less can we rest upon the 'economic harmonies;' and the better we understand the true function of the 'market,' in its widest sense, the more fully shall we realize that it has never been left to itself, and the more deeply shall we feel that it never must be."[34] The external ethical position implied here is reaffirmed in *Common Sense* with such comments as the following:

> But what are my purposes, immediate and ultimate? And what are the purposes of others which serve? And what views have I and they as to the suitable means of accomplishing those ends? These are the questions on which the health and vigor of a community depend, and the economic forces, as such, take no account of them . . . It is idle to assume that ethically desirable results will necessarily be produced by an ethically indifferent instrument, and it is foolish to make the economic relation an idol as it is to make it a bogey . . . When we draw the seductive picture of "economic harmony" in which every one is "helping" some one else and making himself "useful" to him, we insensibly allow the idea of "help" to smuggle in with its ethical and sentimental associations that are strongly contraband.[35]

Wicksteed goes on to cite the following list of "destructive and pernicious" ends that the free market serves: huge industries of war, the floating of bubble companies, the efforts of one business to choke those of others, the poppy culture in China and India, and the gin palaces and distilleries at home.[36] He concludes that "the catholicity of the economic relation extends far enough in either direction to embrace both heaven and hell."[37] The point needing emphasis, and one favored by Hayek, is that externally derived criteria cannot coexist with the logic-of-choice methodological framework; therefore, as Buchanan contends, it is self-contradictory to talk about economics as a "science of choice."[38]

To rectify the problem that we may see (as Wicksteed saw) with what emerges in a free market, constrained only by rules of just conduct, we must have controls that, in turn, lead to the conclusion that theories must be predictive. However, as we have seen, predictive theories that go beyond the dictates of a logic of choice restrict (that is, specify what are the main components of) the utility function of the economic actor, and it seems reasonable that the greater specificity we desire in prediction, the more concerned we must be with detailed patterns of behavior, the more specific the components of the utility function must be. However, in the process of developing the predictability of our theories, we lose their descriptive power, meaning that the theories become a less satisfactory way of describing the human experience. Becker's work is a case in point. His theory of human interaction provides us with testable hypotheses that we once did not have. However, it is also very easy to describe his matrix algebra as a "caricature" of family or small-group experience in general or to complain, as Officer and Stiefel do in their review article, that such analysis omits the effect of "raw emotion" in determining people's behavior.

The point, however, is that we cannot have it both ways: There are trade-offs between the predictive and descriptive relevance of theories as more detailed control is sought; there is a trade-off between the relative precision of a theoretical prediction and the accuracy with which it describes our everyday experience. There is a denial, at least in part, of the creative consciousness of individuals; this is simply because predictive theories in the Becker tradition require that goods be objectively specified, which leaves little room for raw emotions. Indeed, once the good that people are assumed to maximize is specified and the nature of the demand curve and cost function are defined, the theory becomes totally deterministic: The curves then become the theoretical equivalent of the walls of the rat maze through which the individual must run.

B.F. Skinner's deterministic theory represents the extreme to which science must go if it is to take on the detailed management of individual behavior. Skinner does not merely wish to control "patterns of behavior;" rather he wishes to develop a technology of behavior that will enable the controller to elicit very specific responses from those who are controlled.[39] To do this, Skinner must totally deny the subjective and the Wicksteedian logic of choice. Understandably, he is forced to deny, to dispense with, the "prescientific" concepts of will, creative consciousness, and freedom. In their places, he substitutes a totally deterministic theory of behavior, which will "guide" people in pursuit of the "survival of the culture," the ultimate goal in the Skinner view of the world. (Only heaven and Skinner know what is meant by the "survival of the culture.") To the unsympathetic judge, there seems to be only a semantic difference between much current economic analysis and the analysis of modern Skinnerians: Because individual preferences are given, held constant, and virtually all of the discussion centers on the "constraints" and changes in them, talk of "costs" and "benefits" in much economic analysis is simply a substitute for discussion of "positive" and "negative" (external) reinforcers in Skinnerian behaviorism.[40] The social welfare function is the much talked about and sought after external criterion; if followed to its logical conclusion, it leads to predictive theory, which in turn requires severe restrictions on individual utility functions. The concepts of a social welfare function and open-ended utility function are conceptually incompatible.

On the Rise of Predictive Science

All that we have said leads to an easily forgotten question: Why only recently, within the past two decades, has there been a flurry of research, such as Becker's, on so many different, nontraditional topics? A part of the answer is, of course, that economists seek to understand, simply for the sake of understanding, social phenomena that they once did not understand. Furthermore, such studies have become a fad; to write and publish an article is easy because few people have had the time to consider the methodological issues raised by the new research and because it is easier to apply old tools to new problem areas, in which the same old general conclusions seem to hold, than to develop new principles or further refine established principles. (The thought of no new principles to uncover is indeed a seductive one.)

However, a complete answer must involve what amounts to speculation on the trend of science. We have, perhaps, become overly infatuated with the novelty of science, assuming that it is the only route to clear thinking and knowledge. To illustrate George Stigler writes:

> The quantitative, or better, empirical study of economic life is the *only* way in which one can get a feeling for the tasks and functioning of the economic system. The completely formal theorist does not know the range or subtlety of the economic problems that arise each day, for a man is not as resourceful or imaginative as a society of men. The formal theorist therefore has a much simplified picture of the world and of the complexity of the scientific theorems required to explain its operations . . . whereas the experienced empirical worker has had the complexities of the economy burned into his soul. [emphasis added][41]

Interestingly, Stigler articulated this position at a time when he was trying to draw a connection between politics and the role of the political economist.

Hayek and Knight, however, would probably emphasize what they may consider to be a more fundamental reason for the rise of much modern economics. Over the past several decades social control of individual behavior has become much more pronounced. Furthermore, attempts to control have become progressively more specific, meaning that government is attempting to take over or manipulate many detailed behavioral outcomes.[42] Because control has become more specific, the need for more predictive theories has grown, and ever more specific (and debatable) arguments have been introduced into the individual's utility function. The demands of social policy, in other words, have required the scientific community of economists to accept more specific, but less realistic, descriptions of behavior. It means that we have been induced to accept theoretical models that have taken on the appearance of a "Skinnerian box," with little room for the creative consciousness as a viable social force.[43] This is not meant to suggest that these changes are inherently "bad," only that the intent of science has changed in response to strong social forces.

Concluding Comments

This discussion has been wide-ranging, but several obvious conclusions can be drawn. First, the methodological boundaries of economic analysis are not firmly fixed features on a single intellectual plane. The discipline operates on several planes, which we have discussed as the logic of choice, the abstract science of behavior, and the predictive science of behavior. Furthermore, the appropriate plane and the boundaries of the different planes depend, in part, on the world view of the author. Hayek and Knight are both primarily concerned with illuminating the "spontaneous order" that can emerge when just rules of conduct are established. They have only contempt for efforts to manipulate detailed behavioral outcomes; they see such efforts as an affront to basic freedoms and destructive of the justice of the abstract rules of conduct within which the spontaneous order can emerge. In addition, Knight, in particular, doubts that much behavior, although purposeful, is rational in the conventional economic sense of that term. For these reasons, Hayek and Knight would disdain much modern economic analysis. On the other hand, many contemporary economists are not reluctant to use an externally derived criterion to evaluate and alter concrete behavioral outcomes. Their concern is not so much with the broad outlines of a just and long-term social organization, but with seeking expedient solutions to present problems. Their world view is formalized in the concept of the social welfare function, the truth function, and specifically espoused social goals and in their models, which yield empirically refutable hypotheses. Wicksteed, presumably, would be quite comfortable with much current economic work.

In closing, a facet of our inquiry relating to the aesthetic as opposed to the methodological boundaries of economics needs to be noted. Knight warns that, beyond some point, there is a trade-off between understanding and appreciation of the human processes that social scientists attempt to explore; that is, the mechanics of science too easily become transformed in the mind of the person using them into the human processes themselves, as opposed to a representation of them. He writes: "In creation and control as in appreciation, there is more or less conflict between understanding and enjoying. We strive to understand the how and why of our actions, to analyze the technique; and yet when this process is carried too far, and becomes altogether a matter of routine manipulation of means to produce an effect preconceived and foreseen, there is a loss of interest in the action."[44] Similar to specialists in literature who study the metrical structure of poetry until they can no longer appreciate the "how" or the meaning of the poems, economists who try to consider *all* human actions, their's as well as others', may be in danger of failing to experience much of what they seek to understand. Their abstractions, formed into models, may then be nothing more than personal fantasies only remotely connected to the real world.

Notes

1. Admittedly, many of these new areas of inquiry were of considerable interest to economists as far back as Adam Smith; on the other hand, much of the research in these areas has been undertaken without reference to or knowledge of the interests and contributions of much earlier writers.

2. Gary S. Becker, *The Economic Approach to Human Behavior* (Chicago: University of Chicago Press, 1976), p. 8.

3. John Rawls, *A Theory of Justice* (Cambridge, Mass.: Harvard University Press, 1971).

4. Anthony Heath, *Rational Choice and Social Exchange: A Critique of Exchange Theory* (Cambridge: University Press, 1976).

5. John H. Kagel, Raymond C. Batallio, Howard Kachlin, and Leonard Green, "Demand Curves for Animal Consumers," *Quarterly Journal of Economics,* February 1981, pp. 1–16.

6. Richard B. McKenzie and Gordon Tullock, *The New World of Economics: Explorations into the Human Experience* (Homewood, Ill.: Richard D. Irwin, 1981).

7. In their review article, Lawrence Officer and Leanna Stiefel leveled a number of criticisms against the approach and methodology used in *The New World* and, by comment and inference, against the methodology used in many other current economic works. (Lawrence H. Officer and Leanna Stiefel, "The New World of Economics: A Review Article," *Journal of Economic Issues* 10 [March 1976]: 149–58) Indeed, the *Journal of Economic Issues* has carried a number of articles critical of the methodological tradition represented by these new areas of study (see the December 1975 and March 1976 issues of the *Journal of Economic Issues*). Obviously, the Officer and Stiefel review is of more direct concern to me. On the other hand, their review reveals the difficulty of successful communication between authors and reviewers when deep paradigmatic differences separate them; on the other hand, it

has caused me to rethink some basic methodological issues and was the immediate stimulus for this essay.

8. Officer and Stiefel, "The New World," p. 157.

9. Ibid., pp. 152–54.

10. Philip H. Wicksteed, *The Common Sense of Political Economy*, vol. 1 (New York: Augustus M. Kelley, 1967), p. 3.

11. Ibid., p. 161.

12. Ibid., vol. 2, p. 776.

13. Ibid., vol. 1, p. 32.

14. Ibid., vol. 2, p. 780.

15. Ibid., vol. 1, p. 159.

16. Armen A. Alchian and William R. Allen, *University Economics: Elements of Inquiry* (Belmont, Calif.: Wadsworth Publishing, 1972), p. 21.

17. James M. Buchanan, "Is Economics a Science of Choice?" in *Roads to Freedom*, Erich Streissler, ed. (London: Routledge and Kegan Paul, 1969), pp. 47–64.

18. Actually, Wicksteed does not assume that all behavior is purposeful. On several occasions he mentions behavior that is determined or irrational: "A great part of our conduct is impulsive and a great part unreflecting; and when we reflect, our choice is often unrational. In all these cases, however, the principle of price is active." (*Common Sense*, vol. 1, pp. 28–29)

19. Friedrich A. Hayek, *Law, Legislation, and Liberty: The Mirage of Social Justice*, vol. 2 (Chicago: University of Chicago Press, 1976).

20. Hayek, *Law, Legislation, and Liberty*, vols. 1–3 (vol. 3 had not been published at this writing).

21. Milton Friedman, "The Methodology of Positive Economics," *Essays in Positive Economics* (Chicago: University of Chicago Press, 1976).

22. James M. Buchanan, "Reflection on the Alchian Method of Economic Analysis," unpublished draft (Bracksburg: Center for the Study of Public Choice, Virginia Polytechnic Institute and State University, 1969).

23. Ibid.

24. In the latter part of *Common Sense*, Wicksteed becomes very concerned with how people *should* behave and therefore becomes less concerned with economics as a predictive science.

25. Wicksteed, *Common Sense*, p. 184.

26. Friedrich A. Hayek, "Degrees of Explanation," *Studies in Philosophy, Politics and Economics* (Chicago: University of Chicago Press, 1967), pp. 3–21.

27. Hayek, *Law, Legislation, and Liberty*, vol. 2, p. 8.

28. In reference to the functional importance of ignorance in drawing up just rules of social organization, Hayek writes: "That it is thus ignorance of the future outcome which makes possible agreement on rules which serve as a common means for a variety of purposes is recognized by the practice in many instances of deliberately making the outcome unpredictable in order to make agreement on the procedure possible: whenever we agree on drawing lots we deliberately substitute equal chances of the different parties for the certainty as to which of them will benefit from the outcome" (*Law, Legislation, and Liberty*, vol. 2., p. 4). For further elaboration of the connection between ignorance and social justice in general, see especially chapters 1 and 3 of this book by Hayek. For Hayek and Knight's reservations on the usefulness of economics as a predictive science, see Friedrich A. Hayek, "Economics and Knowledge" and "The Facts of the Social Sciences," *Individualism and Economic Order* (Chicago: University of Chicago Press, 1948), pp. 33–76; Hayek, "Degrees of Explanation;" and Frank H. Knight, "The Limitations of Scientific Method in Economics," *The Ethics of Competition and Other Essays* (New York: Harper and Brothers, 1935), pp. 105–14.

29. Knight, "Limitations of Scientific Method," p. 105.

30. Ibid.

31. The model of behavior at this level may say very little, but it has the quality of ambiguity that is so desirable in political statements. And, we must confess, the *process* as opposed to the *ideal* of science has political elements.

32. Ibid., p. 107. Even Officer and Stiefel were resistant to our using the logic of choice to explain or describe a part of people's sexual behavior. They write: "What is gained by such an analysis? The usual criteria for evaluating an economic theory involve the value of the increased understanding in predicting, *controlling,* or accepting social phenomena" [emphasis added]. Since so much scientific analysis is organized for developing control, it is understandable that Officer and Stiefel felt the analysis had some higher purpose than it really did. Imbued with the "practical" dictates of science, they would not, without criticism, allow us to introduce a little humor into our book.

33. Hayek, *Law, Legislation, and Liberty,* vol. 2., chap. 3.

34. Wicksteed, *Common Sense,* vol. 2., p. 783.

35. Ibid., vol. 1, pp. 184–85.

36. Ibid., p. 185.

37. Ibid.

38. Buchanan, "Is Economics a Science of Choice?" Robert Mundel begins the preface to his book *Man and Economics* with this statement: "Economics is the science of choice" ([New York: McGraw-Hill, 1968], p. ii).

39. See, for example, B.F. Skinner, *Beyond Freedom and Dignity* (New York: Bantam Books, 1971).

40. I am indebted to my colleague Robert Staaf for making clear the similarity of Skinner and much modern economic discussion. Indeed, Becker does explicitly assume given preferences and admits that his analysis concerns changes in constraints. See Becker, *The Economic Approach.* When the preferences are given, a creative consciousness from that point on is denied, and the analysis does become deterministic.

41. George J. Stigler, "The Politics of Political Economists," *Quarterly Journal of Economics* 73 (November 1959): 529–30.

42. A column in the Washington *Post,* 29 January 1977, p. A15, by Colman McCarthy recently began with this question: "What kind of family policy will be advanced by the Carter administration?" Such a question cannot be reasonably asked within a logic of choice methodological framework.

43. Hayek contends that more people have become more concerned with detailed social policy because many have become a part of large corporate and government organizations, which, by their nature, must pursue a given "hierarchy of ends":

> One reason why in recent times we have seen a strong revival of organizational thinking and a decline in the understanding of the operation of the market order is that an ever growing proportion of the members of society work as members of large organizations and find their horizon of comprehension limited to what is required by the internal structure of such organizations. While the peasant and independent craftsman, the merchant and the journeyman, were familiar with the market and, even if they did not understand its operations, had come to accept its dictates as the natural course of things, the growth of big enterprise and of great administrative bureaucracies has brought it about that an ever increasing part of the people spend their whole working life as members of large organizations, and are led to think wholly in terms of the requirements of the organizational form of life. [*Law, Legislation, and Liberty,* vol. 2, p. 134]

The organizational way of thinking, according to Hayek, increases the demand for social control and, as we have stated, the logical basis for predictive theories of the Beckerian type.

44. Knight, "Limitations of Scientific Method," p. 107.

3 THE NONRATIONAL DOMAIN AND THE LIMITS OF ECONOMIC ANALYSIS

> *Chanting the square deific, out of the One advancing out of the sides*
> *Out of the old and new, out of the square entirely devine*
> *Solid, four sided, (all sides needed) from this side*
> *Jehovah am I*

> — Walt Whitman
> "Chanting the Square Deific"

The purpose of this chapter is not to downgrade nor to extol the virtue of economic analysis, but rather to reflect on its limitations. In these times, given much professional talk of the expanding domain of economic science and an inclination on the part of some economists to claim that economic analysis has no boundaries, my purpose may seem unusual.[1] My concern is not that we economists have said nothing, but that we have lost sight of the limitations of our methods and, thereby, the limited applicability of the conclusions that have been drawn. More specifically, in much modern discussion, economists seem to have made an unrecognized intellectual leap from assuming that the individual has a rational capacity to assuming that *all* individual behavior has a rational foundation and is therefore subject to logical discourse.

We know explicitly what is meant by *rational* and, its contradistinction, *irrational* behavior, but we apparently have only a vague appreciation for what is meant by *nonrational* behavior, if we recognize its existence at all. A reasonable conclusion to be drawn from the tone of much economic analysis is that the nonrational domain of human behavior is either an empty set or is a set of human actions and reactions that is best characterized by various forms of behavioralism

This is a revised version of an article that appeared in the July 1979 issue of *Southern Economic Journal*. Reprinted with permission of the publisher.

in psychology. Needless to say, an objective of this chapter is to consider the meaning of nonrational behavior and how its existence places an important limitation on the scope and value of economic inquiry.

Because Frank Knight clarified the nonrational dimensions of the human process, I must lean heavily on his work. In fact, in all that I say here, I seek to establish a Knightian methodological perspective from which to evaluate much current study. I argue that economists must temper their professional enthusiasm for the work they undertake and reacquire a balance among modes of inquiry. Perhaps Knight foretold the trend of the discipline more than thirty years ago:

> The great need of the hour in the social sciences field as a whole is for an understanding of the nature of the material, the problems and the possibilities. Only on the basis of such an understanding can we expect so to define our concepts and choose our methods as to avoid not merely waste of energy, but the production of consequences which are positively evil. In the field of social policy, the pernicious notion of instrumentalism, resting on the claim or assumption of a parallelism between social and natural sciences, is actually one of the most serious of the sources of the danger which threaten destruction to the values of what we have called civilization.[2]

Later, Knight follows with:

> As soon as we look concretely and realistically at the problem of getting the knowledge we actually want, . . . we confront the simple fact that our subject matter has to be interpreted in terms of a highly pluralistic system of conceptions or categories . . . Men "exist," so to speak, in several different universes of reality, between which philosophy has so far made no adequate thought bridge, and does not seem to be in the way of doing so.[3]

Admittedly, my arguments are based on an assumed attitude among economists, a kind of implicit tone that pervades much economic discussion. I realize I run the risk of misinterpreting the work of others and of building my arguments of straw. However, having been a party to the popularization, if not development, of some small portion of modern economic discussion, I think I have firsthand knowledge of the intellectual crevasses that have been and are being crossed. Because he is the undisputed leader of the "economic imperialists," I begin with a review of the methodological position of Gary Becker and proceed to a critique of the "new" behavioralism developed by Gary Becker and George Stigler. I argue that a form of Skinnerianism, in which will and freedom are explicitly denied, is the extreme logical derivative of the assumption of the full rationality of human behavior, and that this conflicts with the spirit of assumed rationality.

The Perceived Scope of the Economic Method

After years of applying economic principles to discrimination, human capital, marriage and the family, fertility, and interpersonal relationships in general, Gary

Becker has concluded, as noted in chapter 2, that economic analysis incorporates ''a comprehensive approach'' to the study of human behavior, including the behavior of ''rich or poor persons, adults or children, brilliant or stupid persons, patients or therapists, businessmen or politicians, teachers or students.''[4] Although he never explicitly says so, one comes away from reading Becker with the strong impression that he believes there is no area of human behavior that is not amenable to economic analysis. The only possible exceptions are random actions and those actions predetermined in a Skinnerian sense by environmental and genetic forces. Random behavior can be treated *as if* it has an economic foundation because, in large group settings, it follows the same pattern as economic behavior; that is, random responses on average will follow the path of a downward sloping demand curve when prices change.[5]

In all his work Becker assumes that people are rational, which in simple terms means that people know what they want, are able to order their wants from most preferred to least preferred, and are able to act consistently on the basis of that ordering so as to maximize some general welfare notion such as utility, which Becker often calls ''full income.'' If people are not in fact rational in all their endeavors, then, for theoretical purposes, they can be treated *as if* they are. That is the essence of the foundation of Beckerian economics. The distinction between rationality in fact and rationality in theory is blurred; it is a distinction that need not and, for that matter, cannot be made.

The Beckerian position is tantamount to assuming full or complete rationality; the analysis will follow the same course even if people are not fully rational. The possibilities of miscalculation and error are simply introduced as probabilities of success, which are used to discount appropriately the utility levels attached to success. Rational people are assumed to know what these probabilities are. If they do not, they will seek some optimal level of information on the matter; this optimum is dictated by the known costs and benefits of acquiring the information. Uncertainty, as opposed to the insurable risk, is simply not a part of the Beckerian frames of reference; the ''knowns'' are the benchmarks of consciousness and the efficiency of outcomes.

In an article in the *American Economic Review*, Becker, in collaboration with George Stigler, takes a further step toward a completely behavioralistic conception of human action.[6] In that article, Stigler and Becker attempt to show how tastes can be excluded all together from theoretical discussion. They write, ''Our title [De Gustibus Non Est Disbutandum'']''[7] seems to us to be capable of another and preferable interpretation: That tastes neither change capriciously nor differ importantly between people. On this interpretation one does not argue over tastes for the same reason that one does not argue over the Rocky Mountains — both are there, will be there next year, too, and are the same to all people.''[8] This position may seem extreme to those who consider tastes to be decidedly human and individual and to those who are reluctant to make interpersonal utility comparisons. However, Becker and Stigler take this position because they wish to see how much human behavior can be explained by the "subtle" but objective differences in incomes and prices that confront different people. If we accept tastes as given, or as "data," to use the Stigler-Becker term, and focus solely on the constraints that face individual utility maximizers, then *all* behavior is set within the rationalistic framework; there is no nonrational domain.

Contrary to what is implied, the analysis in the Stigler-Becker mode loses all pretense of dealing with choice as that term is commonly understood. Stigler-Beckerian economics is not a "science of choice."[9] Rather, it is a totally deterministic theory of behavior; to use James Buchanan's classification scheme, it is (at this level of analysis) an "abstract theory of behavior" as opposed to a "logic of choice," a methodological distinction briefly developed in chapter 2.[10] In the Stigler-Becker model, tastes (or preferences), presumably described by conventional indifference maps, are derived externally from the model. Tastes, in other words, are given; so are the constraints. Neither is a matter of subjective determination. The subject in the analysis does not "choose" to operate at the point of tangency between the highest attainable indifference curve and the transformation curve, but is at the point of tangency by specification of the model. Once the preferences and constraints are specified, as they are in the Stigler-Becker model, a computer, which we may add has no distinctly human qualities, can be substituted for the presumed chooser in the model. Further, nothing in the Stigler-Becker model remotely resembles free will, a concept so much a part of the ideological base of neoclassical economists like Stigler and Becker. Constrained on all sides, both internally and externally, the economic actor's actions are subject to mathematical manipulation. As Frank Knight would suggest, the person at center stage in the Stigler-Becker framework is not a problem solver, although the semantics of problem solving are used; all the problems are solved by prior specification of the model. The model allows us to specify the nature of the solution to a nonexistent problem.

Note the unrecognized intellectual crevasse that Stigler and Becker have crossed. True enough, they are intent on using the "logic of choice," which is fundamental to economic theory. Indeed, indifference curve analysis is a useful way of representing a logic of choice when the X and Y axes are left undefined or are merely replaced by examples of goods that may be, but not necessarily are, wanted by the chooser. In this setting the individual chooser is left to identify what the "goods" are, what the labels on the axes should be, and the structure of his own preference mapping. However, when those X's and Y's are replaced by specific, objectively identified goods, such as "music appreciation human capital" or "euphoria from drugs," goods in the Stigler-Becker discussion, the chooser no longer has a choice. Everything is then objective; all is given external to the choosing process.

The similarities are striking between the economic model of Stigler-Becker and the behavioralistic model of Skinner as represented in *Beyond Freedom and*

Dignity.[11] As noted previously, the costs and benefits of Stigler-Becker are semantic substitutes for the positive and negative reinforcers of Skinner, and the Stigler-Becker concept of a self-enlarging human capital, in music for example, takes the place of the Skinnerian concept of "shaping."[12] The emphasis of Stigler-Becker is not on how or even if the individual can create new wants or inspire new forms of behavior — that is, act upon, as opposed to being acted on by, external constraints; the emphasis is on what the external factors are and how they influence or, rather, determine behavior. The comparison of "tastes" to the "Rocky Mountains" is not at all accidental, as strange as that comparison may appear. The Stigler-Becker mode of analysis dictates that such an analogy be drawn.

Stigler and Becker are primarily interested in the predictability of theories. Indeed, to strict positivists such as Stigler and Becker, the accuracy of predictions as determined by empirical evidence developed from models is the sole means of evaluating theories; statements not subject to empirical verification or refutation are simply not meaningful. An interest in the predictability of theories, coupled with a desire to predict people's behavior with regard to specific goods, children (or "child services"), and customs, places strict limitations on the kind of analysis they use. It requires that they turn away from a logic of choice and an abstract theory and toward a deterministic theory of behavior. As we argued in our discussion of Wicksteed's economics in chapter 2, a completely open-ended utility function means the individual economic actor can follow any behavioral pattern; the actor defines the goods and decides how and to what degree to pursue the attainment of those defined goods. With a completely open-ended utility function, the person does not profit maximize, but rather is free to define and follow any number of goals. If all goals are equally admissable, nothing can be predicted because everything is possible. When the methodological framework adopted requires empirical verification, the theory employed is further restricted by the need to collect and manipulate data. The "good" must be externally, objectively, defined, which means that further speculation and restriction on the utility function of the economic actor must be made. The individual must maximize "child services" of a certain kind, the kind of child services on which data are collected, and he is not free to define for himself what he means by "child services." As we have noted before, the individual cannot maximize (or be presumed to maximize) soft-spoken children when the dictates of the empirical analysis call for him to maximize the quantity of children.[13]

Alternately, people are assumed to buy empirically identifiable "apples," to use a distinction employed by Knight. Knight took issue with Friedman's seminal statement of positivism on precisely this distinction.[14] Knight's concerns with strict positivism centered on the implied objectification of all things. In objectively defining goods, the implicit assumption is that there is some identifiable, physical characteristic about the good that gives rise to a mental image of the good to all people: The external characteristics of the good, not the consciousness, determine the image. Accordingly, the techniques of the physical sciences are assumed to be transferable to the social sciences. In this sense, the individual is indeed perceived to be very much like the Rocky Mountains, something responsive to the external forces that hover around it.

Knight was not a radical subjectivist. He recognized the influence of external forces on individual behavior. Further, he conceded that at times the objective characteristics of goods coincided reasonably well with the mental images held by people. In these cases, the techniques are inappropriate and not useful in explaining human action. In his social philosophy, Knight sought a middle ground of "reasonableness" in science.[15] Admittedly, by openly considering the nature of "reasonable science," he opened up a Pandora's box. At the same time, however, his approach focuses professional attention on the boundaries of science in general and economics in particular, one of his professed goals. Before Knight's methodological fuzziness is discarded out of hand, one should ask if his position is any more objectionable than the position that science has no boundaries whatsoever or, the other extreme, that is has no application at all to social behavior.

The Nonrational Domain

Are there limits to economics as a science? Frank Knight gives us a lead in answering that question by implicitly delimiting the nonrational realm. To repeat a quotation stressed in chapter 2, "From a rational or scientific point of view, all practically real problems are problems in economics. The problem of life is to utilize resources 'economically' to make them go as far as possible in the production of desired results."[16] Contrary to the impression left at this point, Knight goes on to say:

> The general theory of economics is therefore simply the rationale of life. — In so far as it has any rationale. The first question in regard to scientific economics is the question of how far life is rational, how far its problems reduce to the form of using given means to achieve given ends. Now this, we shall contend, is not very far; the scientific view of life is a limited and partial view; life is at bottom an exploration in the field of values, an attempt to discover values, rather than on the basis of knowledge of them to produce and enjoy them to the greatest possible extent. We strive to "know ourselves," to find our real wants, more than to get what we want. This fact sets a first and most sweeping limitation to the conception of economics as a science.[17]

As the concept is commonly defined and used, rational behavior presumes that the goods among which we choose and by which the efficiency of the outcome of any subsequent social process is judged are known. Knight simply has pointed out that this is not always the case, nor can it be that we always know what we want. Indeed, he argues that those instances in which we actually know what we want are the exceptions in life. Life is more taken up with defining "wants" than with acting upon given wants. It is, at bottom, experimentation — a trial and error process — in a sea of unknowns. This is the "nonrational domain."[18]

If we acknowledge that wants cannot be established instantaneously, there must be some time-consuming process by which wants are shaped and changed. During this time, although actual choices become entangled, we cannot always choose from among knowns or even quasi-knowns. The problem the utility-maximizing individual faces is often similar, but not identical, to the problem faced by the individual who is set down in the middle of a densely forested mountain range and is told to climb to the highest peak. From where he is he can tell which way is up, but he cannot see the peaks around him and therefore cannot tell whether he should climb to the top of the mountain he is on or go down and try another. Even when he reaches the peak of one mountain he cannot be sure he has reached the highest peak. The individual may know with clarity his overriding goal, but this is not always helpful in guiding the decisions that he must make on a day-to-day basis. In this type of setting, the concept of efficiency (as defined in economics) and the concept of determined solution (in the exante sense) have no relevance because there are no "goods" as reference points. Further, the techniques of economic inquiry, which are so dependent upon defined goods, are inapplicable in this area of human experience, even though resources (physical but with no economic evaluation) are involved.

It is in the nonrational domain that individuals are free to identify and adopt something on the order of the Kantian or Christian (or any other) ethic, which, because of its generalized nature, directs and constrains the process by which other, possibly lower-order, values are formed. It is in the nonrational domain that the individual can rightfully be characterized as *internally* directed as opposed to *externally* directed as in Becker and Skinner behavioralism.[19]

And it is because of the nonrational domain that personal responsibility for actions has any reasonable meaning. In the externally directed world of behavioralism, all action is a response to external forces, and therefore no act can be accurately attributed to the individual actor. In fact, Skinner explicitly argues that personal responsibility is an arcane, prescientific concept that has no meaning in the world of the behavior technologist.[20] Finally, it is in the nonrational domain that give-and-take normative discourse enables us to understand what Paul Tillich was getting at when he wrote of "the courage to be:" It is the courage to affirm one's rational nature itself.[21] Following Tillich, rational behavior cannot exist without the prior, arduous, and time-consuming process of affirming one's rational capacity.[22]

Economic inquiry may be able to penetrate partially the realm of human experience in which values are formed. The subfield of the economics of information has made inroads in this realm. For instance, we may reasonably assume that people have an interest in using their resources efficiently in the search process; they can be expected to acquire some optimum level of information given what they "know" at the start of the search process. However, because an infinite regress lurks in the wings of logical discourse, we cannot deduce that the entire search process is amenable to economic analysis. If one seeks some rationally determined level of information on alternative goods and services, then how does one determine how much information one must seek on that level of information? How do we define the goods on which information is sought when the definition of goods is the object of the search? What is the starting point? How is it determined? How much of life is actually involved in establishing those starting points, especially if we assume, as did von Mises, that "man is [always] eager to substitute a more satisfactory state of affairs for a less satisfactory one,"[23] and that he has an infinite capacity to envision more satisfactory states when any given state is attained. Contrary to the implied contention of Stigler and Becker, tastes do matter, and they matter greatly if we start with the position that they are not given but continuously evolving.[24]

Why must we constantly look for external forces to explain behavior? There are two possible reasons: (1) to increase understanding and (2) to secure control of behavior. Skinner is very open about his intentions. Knight would surely be concerned about the less openly expressed intentions of social scientists in general and economists in particular and would encourage discussion of those intentions.

Nonrationality and the Necessity of Social Interaction

Social science seeks solutions to the independently derived problems from the actual social processes that are under investigation. The solutions are sought in the laboratories and think tanks of the country, not through social interaction. Generally, the problems are relatively simple, and the models used employ basic data — given wants — which are already the product of much social interaction. Therefore, in economists' models much of the complexity of social interaction has already been set aside.

In the work of social scientists, the temptation is ever present to assume that social interaction itself serves no real or useful purpose that cannot be "better" served by social science, if only social scientists are given more resources to conduct their investigations. In short, it is tempting to assume that social interaction is not a mechanism for solving problems. However, once we recognize that much of life involves experimentation and efforts, through interaction with others, to establish what we do want, we see that social interaction is in fact a means for coping with problems that cannot be reduced to a form manipulable with mathematics or computers with the largest of capacities. Models of behavior cannot, therefore, be a substitute for experience, which is a maze of indeterminacy in an exante sense.

From this perspective freedom is necessary not only because it allows people to choose efficiently and seek out the tangency between some ill-conceived indifference curve and budget constraint, but also because it allows people to *define* what they do want. If people do not have the capacity to interact freely, they do not have the capacity to solve complex problems that cannot be solved in any other way, to achieve outcomes that cannot be predicted and determined prior to social interaction. Freedom has far less meaning in a world in which people are fully rational than in a world in which the nonrational domain is recognized and is considered to be an integral part of conscious existence.

As is argued more extensively in a later chapter, the case for the free market is made stronger, not weaker, when the nonrational domain is recognized. In a free market people have the capacity to interact, to establish what they want, what they want to trade, and how they want to trade.[25] The entrepreneur, who following Israel Kirzner can be either a consumer or business person, has the capacity to perceive what is wanted and the difference between the prices of inputs and outputs. In the absence of this entrepreneurial ability, the market loses the driving force of competition. Furthermore, this entrepreneurial function is at least partially outside the rational domain; it is not fully a problem of efficiently utilizing resources to satisfy known wants of market participants, partly because market participants do not always know what they want and are a part of the market process to make that determination. As Kirzner has written, "Entrepreneurship does not consist of grasping a free ten-dollar bill which one has already discovered to be resting in one's hand; it consists in realizing that it is in one's hand and that it is available for the grasping . . . The discovery of profitable opportunities *means the discovery of something obtainable for nothing at all*. No investment is required; the ten-dollar bill is discovered to be already within one's grasp."[26] Kirzner further argues that the role of the entrepreneur is eliminated when there are perfectly competitive markets in which the goods are already defined, when there is perfect information among market participants, and when markets are in equilibrium.

The market facilitates the interaction process of entrepreneurs because, as Hayek has emphasized in all his writings, it reduces the amount of information one needs to interact successfully with others and to grasp profitable opportunities. The market economizes on the nonrational component of behavior, but it by no means eliminates the nonrational component. To do that, the market would have to eliminate a function that it serves.

In making the case for the free market, economists usually assume that all market participants are rational. One possible reason for their assumption is apparently not that they fully believe it, but to make the case for the market using an unfavorable set of conditions so that their audience will see the case is made even stronger when those conditions are relaxed.

Concluding Comments

A nonrational domain implies some indeterminacy in behavior; it places all further discussion outside the scope of science, as Stigler and Becker emphasize. However, it does not follow that because an issue is outside the scope of science, it does not matter. It is this indeterminacy of social interaction that Knight and others have called ''uncertainty'' and that necessitates free social interaction if individual values are to be formed as well as recognized. Knight argues that it is uncertainty that makes consciousness a meaningful and distinctly human state of being.[27] If all were known to the extent implied or explicitly assumed in much modern economic discussions, calculating machines could be substituted for people and solutions would be found, obviating the need for human interactions and the study of it.

The assumption of rational behavior is clearly less objectionable at some levels of analysis than at others. For example, at the constitutional level where the broad outlines of social institutions are the subject of discussion, people must determine by the nature of the question at issue what they want and devise an explicit ordering of constitutional variables. The efficiency of the emerging consensus can then be judged in terms of these individual orderings. If we are concerned solely with the broad institutional framework of society, we leave room for people to interact and to detemine, in subsequent behavior, what they want and how and what they will trade. Restrictions on persons' utility functions in subsequent behavior are not necessary; future interactions are left constrained but open-ended. On the other hand, if we wish to study specific areas of behavior, as opposed to what Hayek terms ''patterns of outcomes,'' we must define objectively very specific goods; and this requirement alone forces us into deterministic models of human behavior. At the limit, it leaves no room for indeterminacy. It is no wonder, when we seek to explain with economic models very specific behavior, economists tend to raise the ire of people who view nonrational, nondeterminant forms of behavior as dominant in human experience.

Where does the discussion in this chapter lead us, especially those of us who are interested in pushing back the boundaries of economics? In the first place, it suggests that we must pull back from such sweeping positional statements as ''there is no such thing as a free lunch,'' because such statements are not fully descriptive of all human experience. In the nonrational domain, values are in the process of being formed. When the value of an alternative is undefined, nothing can be perceived as being given up when any one thing is done. One cannot characterize what is done as being ''free,'' but neither can it be characterized as having a cost. What is done is done; it is as simple as that.

Further, the methodological techniques of Knight have application to contemporary discussions of economists. At times, Knight pushed the logic of economic man to its limits, drawing whatever conclusions flowed from the model he had set up. However, recognizing that the individual's existence is multidimensional, he pulled back from the rigor of logical discourse to reassert the limited usefulness of the insights acquired. (Knight seems to have always placed stress on both ''limited'' and ''useful'' as characteristics of economics.) As John McKinney has written about Knight's work in a recent article: ''Though Knight's concern is to keep science within an appropriately restricted domain, he does not, like numerous critics of orthodox economics, protest what is often regarded as the economist's attempt to reduce man to mere mechanism, passively reacting to hedonist pleasures and pains. Rather, he seeks, in his role of scientist, to develop rigorously mechanical interpretations of human conduct, and then, as a social philosopher and moralist, impress upon his readers the 'sweeping limitations' which must be placed on such an interpretation.''[28] In the interest of achieving balance in interpreting people's behavior, Knight was willing to run the risk of being called to task for being contradictory. He felt that contradictions were to be expected because human experience is to be fully experienced, but not fully explained or predicted by detached scientific methods. He could not construct the ''intellectual bridges,'' but at the same time he made his discussion of the human predicament plausible, insightful, and enduring. These qualities are best summarized in this passage:

> That ''man is a rational animal'' is one of those interesting statements which do not have to be proved, since the subject admits it. In fact he says so himself; and the objective value of the statement is to be appraised in the light of that fact. It must also be viewed in the light of other statements ''man'' makes about himself. By the same authority, he is also a groping ignoramus, a fool, and a miserable sinner, quite unworthy of redemption. The list of opposite characteristics could be indefinitely extended, and all the statements would be true, in varying degree and numerous interpretations. But by the same token each is false or, taken singly and alone, is an exaggeration and over-simplication.[29]

Notes

1. It may appear especially unusual for me to examine the limitation of economic analysis since I have, in much of my writing in the past few years, attempted to see how far the boundaries of economic can be stretched (Richard B. McKenzie and Gordon Tullock, *The New World of Economics* [Homewood, Ill: Richard D. Irwin, 1975, 1978, and 1981]). My purpose here, however, is not to propose that economists discard what they have accomplished. I remain confident of the *limited* usefulness of economic analysis in many unconventional areas, such as crime, marriage, and the family.

2. Frank H. Knight, "Fact and Values in Social Science," *Freedom and Reform: Essays in Economics and Social Philosophy* (Port Washington, N.Y.: Kennikat Press, 1969 [1947]), p. 25.

3. Ibid., p. 230.

4. Gary S. Becker, *The Economic Approach to Human Behavior* (Chicago: University of Chicago Press, 1976), p. 8.

5. See Gary S. Becker, *Economic Theory* (New York: Alfred Knopf, 1971).

6. George J. Stigler and Gary S. Becker, "De Gustibus Non Est Disputandum," *American Economic Review*, March 1977, pp. 76–90.

7. This translates as "There is No Quarreling Over Tastes."

8. Stigler and Becker, "De Gustibus," p. 76.

9. Many economists, like Robert Mundel, protest that "Economics is the science of choice" (Robert A. Mundel, *Man and Economics* [New York: McGraw-Hill, 1968]), p. v.

10. See James Buchanan, "Is Economics a Science of Choice?" *Roads to Freedom: Essays in Honour of Friedrich A. Von Hayek* (London: Routledge and Kegan Paul, n.d.).

11. B.F. Skinner, *Beyond Freedom and Dignity* (New York: Bantam Books, 1971).

12. Stigler and Becker, "De Gustibus," pp. 77–81.

13. See chapter 2.

14. Milton Friedman, "The Methodology of Positive Economics," *Essays in Positive Economics* (Chicago: University of Chicago Press, 1953), pp. 3–46.

15. As told to me by James M. Buchanan, a student of Knight, who at the time of the conversation was reflecting on Knight's class lectures.

16. Frank H. Knight, "The Limitations of Scientific Methods in Economics," *The Ethics of Competition and Other Essays* (New York: Harper and Row, 1936), p. 105.

17. Ibid.

18. The nonrational behavior with which this chapter is concerned has characteristics of, but is not fully compatible with, the "nonlogical" behavior discussed at length by Pareto in his sociological treatise (Vilfredo Pareto, *The Mind and Society* [New York: Harcourt Brace and Co., 1935]). To Pareto nonlogical actions are actions for which the objective end ("as it is in reality") differs from its subjective purpose ("as it presents itself to the mind of this or that human being"). Logical actions are those actions for which means and ends are connected both subjectively and objectively. Rational behavior is different: It requires that only the subjectively perceived ends and means be logically linked. In our usage here, nonrational behavior includes those actions for which the ends are not perceived at all or perceived with clarity. For an exposition of Pareto's concept of nonlogical actions and why Pareto felt such actions do not weaken the applicability of scientific techniques to social behavior, see Vincent J. Tanascio, *Pareto's Methodological Approach to Economics* (Chapel Hill: University of North Carolina Press, 1968).

19. I am indebted to Richard Wagner for making clear to me the significance of the distinction between internally and externally directed behavior.

20. On this point Skinner writes, "The hypothesis that man is not free is essential to the application of scientific method to the study of human behavior. The free inner man who is held responsible for the behavior of the external biological organism is only a prescientific substitute for the kinds of causes which are discovered in the course of a scientific analysis." (*Science and Human Behavior* [New York: Macmillan, 1953], p. 447).

21. Paul Tillich, *The Courage to Be* (New Haven, Conn.: Yale University Press, 1952).

22. Although he defines the phrase in several different ways throughout the book, Tillich's central expression of the concept is as follows: "The courage to be is the courage to affirm our own rational nature, in spite of everything in us that conflicts with its union with the rational nature of being itself" (ibid., p. 13). Later, Tillich defines "the courage to be" as an expression of faith.

23. Ludwig von Mises, *Human Action: A Treatise on Economics* (New Haven, Ct.: Yale University Press, 1949).

24. Actually the Stigler and Becker position on tastes is unclear; they may have merely renamed tastes as a form of human capital.

25. Israel M. Kirzner, *Competition and Entrepreneurship* (Chicago: University of Chicago Press, 1973).

26. Ibid., pp. 47–48.

27. Frank H. Knight, *Risk, Uncertainty, and Profit* (New York: Augustus M. Kelly, 1951 [1921]).

28. John McKinney, "Frank H. Knight on Uncertainty and Rational Action," *Southern Economic Journal*, April 1977, pp. 1438–52.

29. Frank H. Knight, "The Planful Act: The Possibilities and Limitation of Collective Rationality," *Freedom and Reform: Essays in Social Philosophy*, p. 341.

4 THE NEOCLASSICISTS vs. THE AUSTRIANS:

A Partial Reconciliation of Competing World Views

Economists of the neoclassical-Chicago and Austrian schools of thought are usually vociferous defenders of individual freedom, critics of government, developers of market economics, and believers in rational discourse as a means of seeking solutions to observed social concerns. However, instead of claiming intellectual kinship based on shared values and theoretical premises, members of both schools frequently dismiss (in private) one another as muddleheaded or even perverse in their theoretical attachments.

Traditional neoclassical economic literature is largely devoid of references to Austrian contributions, suggesting the extent to which Austrian economics is ignored in graduate programs and overlooked in literature searches. When confronted by an Austrian economist, the first impulse of many neoclassical economists must be to ask, quite seriously, "What *is* Austrian economics?" Milton Friedman once quipped at a meeting of Austrian economists that "there is no Austrian economics — only good economics and bad economics;" but he added that the important contributions of Austrian economics could reasonably be incorporated into the mainstream of economic thought.[1]

This is a revised version of an article that appeared in the July 1980 issue of *Southern Economic Journal*. Reprinted with permission of the publisher.

Aside from a few luminaries, such as Friedrich Hayek, most contemporary Austrians were trained in neoclassical orthodoxy. They know the form and substance of neoclassical analysis. Indeed, they frequently use neoclassical economics as a "whipping boy" in their essays and/or as the raison d'etre for Austrian economics. Austrians typically refer to positive economics — and positivism in general — as "scientism," expressing disdain for what they believe is a gross misapplication of scientific methods to social problems. Perturbed with the drift of modern social science, Hayek notes in his Nobel lecture:

> Economists are at this moment called upon to say how to extricate the free world from the serious threat of accelerating inflation which, it must be admitted, has been brought about by policies which the majority of economists recommended and even urged government to pursue. We have at the moment little cause for pride: as a profession we have made a mess of things. It seems to be this failure of the economists to guide policy more successfully is closely connected with their propensity to imitate as closely as possible the procedure of the brilliantly successful physical sciences — an attempt which in our field may lead to outright error. It is an approach which has come to be described as the "scientific" attitude — an attitude which, as I defined it some thirty years ago, "is decidedly unscientific in the true sense of the word, since it involves a mechanical and uncritical application of habits of thought to fields different from those in which they have been formed."[2]

Hayek effectively condemns positive, neoclassical economics for giving rise to what he calls the "pretense of knowledge," the appearance of understanding the world about us.

The central purpose of this chapter is to explore the representative positions of the two schools of thought; to locate major points of differences that have polarized economists with similar, if not identical, ideological and policy positions; and to suggest a partial reconciliation of what both sides regard as inimical views. The analysis will concentrate on three key philosophical and theoretical points of separation between the neoclassicists, as represented by Milton Friedman, and Austrians, as represented by Friedrich Hayek: (1) the nature of economics as a discipline, (2) the predictability of human action, and (3) the nature and purpose of theory. The analysis suggests that when neoclassical and Austrian economics are laid bare by the sharpness of contrast, a great deal of compatibility in purpose and policy conclusions are evident. This compatibility, rather than irreconcilable differences, is the focus of this chapter.

The Nature of the Discipline

Neoclassical economics is, in the main, wedded to "Robbinsian" maximizing behavior, which posits a fundamental distinction and conflict between the internal subjective world of the individual and the external objective world in which the individual pursues personal goals. Neoclassical economics presumes that the objective external world exists independently of the subjective. "Economics," wrote Lionel Robbins in 1930, "is the science which studies human behavior as a relationship between ends and scarce means which have alternative uses."[3] *The* "economic problem" emerges when the individual pursues subjectively established interests by objective external means. "Economizing behavior" is, almost by definition, the individual's natural response to the personal "problem" that emerges. Economics, in the neoclassical view of the world, has no application to those areas of human existence in which means are not scarce relative to ends. However, as Wicksteed first argued in *Common Sense* and noted earlier in this book, the ends-means conflict is believed to be pervasive, encompassing such "heterogeneous indulgences" as virtue, wisdom, sagacity, prudence, honor, success, literature, sex, art, education, and spiritual enjoyment.[4] The burgeoning literature in applied microeconomic theory clearly suggests the limits, or perhaps the lack of limits, that is perceived for neoclassical economic analysis (see chapter 1).

In several important respects, Robbin's characterization of economics captures and expresses, as is intended, the dominant views of neoclassicists toward acceptable social research methods. First, in the Robbinsian view of the world, the individual, who is the object of analysis, is conceived as a "problem solver." And the problem is as much prescribed by external constraints as by internal desires: Constraints (graphically illustrated by a transformation curve or budget line) are conceptually independent of values (graphically illustrated by indifference curves); values do not determine the *existence* of constraints. Constraints are simply a part of the objective reality, meaning they can be identified by the researcher (economist) who, detached from the maximizing process, conducts the analysis.

Second, the notions of problem solving and maximizing behavior presuppose "solutions." Given the neoclassicist's presumption of an objective reality, which embodies outcomes as well as constraints, direct observation (and measurement) of "solutions" is also presupposed. If it can be agreed at the start that there is an objective quality to the world, then it follows that much of what is observed in the real world can, by an implied social agreement within the scientific community, be categorized as relevant or irrelevant to the maximization process. It also follows that scientific-economic predictions can be subjected to empirical test: Because of the objective character of the world, we know or can agree on what is or is not an outcome — an objective event — that is predicted. To suggest that theoretical predictions cannot be evaluated with reference to real-world events is a denial of a basic tenet in neoclassical economics: An objective reality is established independently of values of maximizing individuals and researchers.

Neoclassicists, therefore, presume that the statement "an apple is an apple" has some meaning, and social agreement within the community of researchers as to what does and does not constitute an apple gives meaning to the statement. The values people place on apples cannot be observed directly, but the apples themselves can, by the sheer meaning of objective reality, be segmented from other objects like oranges and can be counted. Objective measurement of anything is not a logical deduction, but a presumption of neoclassical science. Neoclassicists, in this regard, are pragmatists, willing to take as given the ability of people to categorize, albeit imperfectly, real-world events and outcomes, much like physical scientists are able to do. To the neoclassicists, social outcomes are not categorically different, as far as their objectivity is concerned, from the outcomes of physical processes. Predictions in the physical sciences are meaningful solely because people can agree on what does and does not constitute a physical event; the same type of agreement, to the neoclassicists, makes social predictions meaningful. This is what Friedman must have had in mind when he attempted to make the case for the methodological equivalence of positive economics and the physical sciences.[5]

Third, the neoclassicists view the individual actor as standing astride the subjective and objective realms of the world. A presumed function of science — for descriptive completeness, if for no other reason — is to relate in some meaningful way the two realms, to tie the two realms together by some method because individual actions — outcomes — are a consequence of the interaction of the two realms. Again, the pragmatism of the neoclassicists comes through; their world view presupposes consensus on what constitutes objective reality, and reference to "facts," on which people can agree, gives meaning to statements. Indeed, agreement defines, in large measure, the meaningfulness of a statement. No agreement is presumed with reference to subjective evaluation of "goods" because there is no basis for establishing what constitutes agreement. (What is "satisfaction derived from apples"?) However, agreement is possible within the objective world, by the very definition of what is meant by the objective world. Circularity in reasoning is precluded by the exogenous nature of the social agreement on objective reality.

The Austrian conception of the nature and scope of economics differs, in several important regards, from the neoclassical conception. Like the neoclassicists, the Austrians accept as an article of faith, verified by simple introspection, that people have the capacity to perceive, order, and act upon their preferences.[6] "The term *action*," writes Edwin Dolan, "as used by Austrian theorists, takes on a precise technical sense that is perhaps best understood by contrasting actions with events. An event may be thought of as something that 'just happens' — a change that takes place in the state of the world, such as a rock falling from a cliff and killing Smith. An action, in contrast, is something that happens as a result of purposeful intervention in the 'natural' course of events."[7]

Although Austrians may, if pressed, admit to an objective world, such a conception does not play a central role *in their theoretical structure*. The world is conceived and viewed, almost entirely, through the eyes of the individual actor, one who determines what one wants to do and does it. With regard to "objective reality," two views can be distinguished. First, to the "radical subjectivist," the subjective defines the objective, meaning that the apple, *for theoretical purposes* at least, does not exist independently of someone's perception of its existence. A person does not seek to consume objective apples but seeks to consume "images of apples." That is, to the radical subjectivist, people buy "things" for various reasons, and the things they do buy, although appearing to be the same "thing," are actually quite different, as different and distinct as are the evaluations people place on the consumption of different units. Hence, counting the number of apples people buy is as untenable as summing up the number of oranges and apples they buy. From this perspective, individual valuation is the sole common denominator of aggregating goods and services that are consumed. This view rules out totally any criteria, external to the exchange process itself, for evaluating exchanges made.

Taking a less extreme position, other Austrians may admit to the existence of an objective reality distinguishable from preferences. However, even this group makes subjective evaluation the centerpiece of theory. Apples may be apples, but apples are consumed under complex circumstances. The circumstances of consumption can vary radically from person to person, so much so that it is unreasonable to assume, as a matter of course, that when a collection of individuals consumes apples they are in fact consuming the same "objective good."

Time is a good and/or resource singled out for special attention by the Austrians. All actions require time, but an hour of time means different things to different people. This is because basic evaluations of time differ and because all actions are guided by subjectively established goals that differ among people. Hours of time cannot be added together for the same reason apples cannot be counted. Similarly, there can be no aggregate measure of, say, a country's capital stock; present value calculations presume a constancy in the standard by which time in the future is valued. "The impracticability of measurement is not due to the lack of technical methods for the establishment of measure. It is due," writes von Mises, "to the absence of constant relations. Economics is not, as . . . positivists repeat again and again, backward because it is not 'quantitative.' It is not quantitative and does not measure because there are no constants."[8]

To the neoclassicists, the ever-present conflict between ends and scarce means is viewed as a "problem" that must be overcome and that has recognizable solutions. To the Austrians, the "problem" defines meaningful existence. Seen from their perspective, pursuit of a "less unsatisfactory" state of affairs can hardly be construed as a problem; if it is, it is a problem to be relished. The "problem" presupposes as much "improvement" as it does "conflict."

Economics, in the Austrian way of thinking, is limited to praxeology, which, according to Rothbard, "is the structure of logical implications of the *fact* that individuals act."[9] The "implications" deduced are not subject to empirical tests because of, as has been noted, the lack of "constants" and because there is simply no need to test the correctness of the implications "since their truth has already been established" by the truth of basic premises and the rules of logic.[10] Austrian economics is restricted to the "logic of choice," in contrast to the "predictive science" of neoclassical economics, to use Buchanan's analytical distinction developed earlier in chapter 2.

As a logic of choice, mathematics, to some Austrians, can make a useful contribution to our understanding of the *pattern* of human actions, as long as the *X*'s and *Y*'s in the formulas are left totally undefined and as long as numerical values for the parameters are left unestimated. Hayek comments:

> I want to avoid giving the impression that I generally reject the mathematical technique that it allows us to describe, by means of algebraic equations, the general character of a pattern even where we are ignorant of the numerical values of those magnitudes; and this has led to a vain search for quantitative or numerical constants.[11]

In conclusion, neoclassical economists tend to view the world as a sequence of "problems" from which they are detached but on which they are called to comment. Their concern with "what is" suggests that they are interested in more than mere abstractions about what might emerge from the interaction of individuals. They perceive themselves as detached problem solvers who are interested in drawing conclusions about specific problems, making policy recommendations in the give-and-take world of politics. They do not wish to engage in normative discussion, but by the same token they seek *objective* criteria by which specific outcomes can be evaluated, if for no other reason than to thwart the misguided efforts and interests of other parties operating within party politics. A test of their analysis is not only the degree to which predictions are found correct but also the degree to which the relevant public *agrees* that real-world measures are reasonable proxies.

Many, but by no means all, Austrian economists, on the other hand, view the world as an emerging and constantly evolving process by which people act and react in pursuit of their individually established interests. The problems that exist are not the problems of the Austrians; the problems that do exist are the problems of the participants in the evolutionary process. Austrians tend to see themselves as spectators of "patterns of outcomes" and as persons who are called upon to comment on the type of institutional-constitutional framework that will permit people to solve their *own* problems that emerge as they seek to improve *their* unsatisfactory state.

In large measure, the views of the neoclassicists and Austrians are complementary, dealing with different perceptions of society and different types of problems. Many Austrians are concerned with basic societal structure, that is, "the constitution of liberty," to use a phrase made popular by Hayek. The neoclassicists, being pragmatists, are concerned with developing a methodology for dealing with social outcomes that can emerge within the basic societal structure. The constitutional structure of society is largely subsumed.

The Predictability of Human Action

The basic positions of the neoclassicists and Austrians on the predictability of human behavior have been stated. Prediction is *a,* if not *the,* centerpiece of positive neoclassical economics.[12] In other words, the "rightness" or "wrongness" of a theory is mainly a "factual" matter that can be established by a series of empirical tests.[13] The neoclassical researcher is presumed to be sufficiently competent to extract from a "complex reality" those "essential" variables and to choose proxy variables that can make a test of the theory meaningful with experience "not yet observed."[14] The inability of the researcher to conduct controlled experiments and the difficulty of the researcher to interpret "evidence" are seen, in the neoclassical world, as mere obstacles in "achieving a reasonably prompt and wide consensus on the conclusions justified by the available evidence. It renders the weeding-out of unsuccessful hypotheses slow and difficult."[15]

Any theoretical statement, unaccompanied by an empirical test of the central hypothesis, is considered by many neoclassicists as "unfinished," at best, and at worst, "fanciful speculations." George Stigler argues that Adam Smith offered his countrymen some "clear and emphatic advice on the proper way to achieve economic prosperity," but Stigler concludes that "the basic role of the scientists in public policy, therefore, is that of establishing the costs and benefits of alternative institutional arrangements. Smith had no professional right to advise England on the Navigation Acts unless he had *evidence* of their effects and the probable effects of their repeal," which according to Stigler Smith did not have. By the same token, "A modern economist has no professional right to advise the federal government to regulate or deregulate the railroads unless he has evidence of the effects of these policies."[16]

Stigler contends that a study of the costs and gains of policy proposals is necessary in order that we may *know* whether the public or private sector can more efficiently accomplish established goals and objectives. The growing insistence among economists for quantification of the costs and gains of policies and for empirical testing of hypotheses has thrown economics into the "threshold of its golden age."[17] Notice that to a neoclassical economist like Stigler what government should do is largely an open question to be decided by cost-benefit analysis; to Austrian economists like Hayek that question is largely closed by an established constitution that dictates the boundaries of government. Stigler can agree with Hayek that government should be "limited," without agreeing with his approach to economics, because all of Stigler's empirical research points to the conclusion that many modern government programs are inefficient.

Austrians (almost) uniformally reject empirical tests for two fundamental reasons: First, the tests are unnecessary. Second, there are no constants to measure and use in empirical tests. Econometric and statistical techniques may have some application in extracting the patterns of history and therefore be useful to the historian interested in explaining what happened and when; but such techniques are totally inapplicable to predicting events "not yet observed." Markets are viewed among Austrians as "spontaneous order" that emerges as people, attempting to pursue their own interest, adjust and readjust their own actions to the actions of others. Because of the learning that occurs as people interact with one another, "complex reality" is never quite the same and cannot therefore be predicted on the basis of past regularities.[18]

The Nature and Purpose of Theory

The conflicting positions of the neoclassicists and many Austrians on the predictability of human actions suggests that the two schools of thought are irrevocably separated to some extent into warring methodological camps. In this section, we consider in more detail the neoclassicists' and Austrians' positions on the nature and purpose of theory. As has been shown above and as will be shown here, the methodological schism between the neoclassicists and Austrians is not nearly as wide as a comparison of basic positions indicates.

To the neoclassicists, theory is an apparatus of the mind, designed to promote "systematic and organized methods of reasoning."[19] By its very nature, theory cannot be a replica of objective reality, because the purpose of theory is, using Kenneth Boulding's words, to condense, abstract, and index "the great buzzing confusion of information that comes from the world around us into a form which we can appreciate and comprehend."[20] Hence, theory cannot be judged in terms of its "realism" because it was never intended to be real and is not real; it is a technique for thinking.

As is well known, neoclassicists go one step further and contend that assumptions underlying a theory can be made purposefully "unreal." For theoreical purposes, people can be assumed to be *completely* rational and markets can be assumed to be perfectly competitive, although they are not and the theoretician *may realize* they are not. The theoretician is presumed to be interested solely in a *workable* model of behavior, and the workability of any model is determined by the extent to which the model makes correct predictions about phenomena "not yet observed." If people are not fully rational, they can be assumed to behave *as if* they are fully rational.

To Friedman and other neoclassicists, a theory is merely a convenient fiction, a rule of thumb, capable of generating predictions that are more often correct than those generated by other convenient fictions. Predictions generated from the workable models of human behavior are the equivalent of explanations. Alan Coddington offers two arguments that may justify the presumed equivalence of predictions and explanation. First, prediction and explanation may be seen as having the same logical structure, leading to the conclusion that predictive accuracy and explanatory power are one and the same concept: "It is interesting to note that Marshall subscribed to the view that explanation is the same as retrospective theory. He maintained that the difference between the two is merely that whereas prediction goes from cause to effect, explanation goes from effect to cause."[21] Second, prediction may be viewed as equivalent to explanatory power because economic analysis is unable to "explain anything in any deep or satisfying sense," and, therefore, we should seek to accomplish "the more modest task of finding generalizations which 'work' (in the sense of having a good predictive performance)."[22]

Austrians are interested in the predictability of theory, but in a limited sense. They are concerned with predicting a "pattern of outcomes" or a "range of possibilities," two phrases frequently employed by Hayek.[23] Theories are more noted for what is not expected than for what is expected. They may not provide us with the types of knowledge that we might like to have; nevertheless, "these theories," Hayek points out, "equip us with ready-made schemes which tell us that when we observe given patterns of phenomena, certain patterns are to be expected but not others. They will show their value through the manner in which the isolated facts, which have been known, will begin to make sense — that is, will fit the *niches* which the theory provides, and only those."[24]

In the Austrian methodological world, predictions concerning patterns of outcome are all that can be expected from the study of social interaction. Social science, in general, and economics, in particular, deal with extraordinarily complex phenomena, so complex that they could not be observed in their entirety even if they could be measured in their entirety. Hence, "where only the most general patterns can be observed in a considerable number of instances, the endeavor to become more 'specific' by further narrowing down our formula may well be a waste of effort; to strive for this in some subjects such as economics has often led to the illegitimate assumption of constants where in fact we have no right to assume the factors in question to be constant."[25] And, "for this reason economic theory is confined to describing kinds of patterns which will appear if certain general conditions are satisfied, but can rarely if ever derive from this knowledge any prediction of specific phenomena."[26]

Even if it were possible to make very precise predictions concerning concrete events that may occur within a pattern of outcomes, many Austrians would appear to argue that such predictions *should not* be made. As we have indicated, Austrians are primarily interested in constructing the broad constitutional framework for a free society within which people are able to pursue their own interest. At the constitutional stage of social development, people's lack of knowledge concerning specific events within the expected pattern of outcomes is the methodological equivalent of Rawl's veil of ignorance, behind which people will devise a constitutional structure that will maximize social welfare by way of maximizing individual freedom. If people could predict specific events within the general pattern of outcomes, the incentives faced by people interested in constructing a "constitution of liberty" will be distorted and the morality and justice of the constitutional framework will be open to question. Furthermore, Austrians fear that prediction capability regarding specific events will lead to control mechanisms that will be misused. And because the predictions are likely to be wrong frequently, the controls will often be misguided. Controls will spawn controls, a central message of Hayek's *Road to Serfdom*.[27]

For hardcore Austrians and neoclassicists, the methodological positions just developed on the nature of theory can, perhaps, never be reconciled satisfactorily. However, for those who do not have vested interests in established positions, partial reconciliation of the two views may, for several reasons, be feasible. In attempting such a reconciliation, it should first be pointed out that theory in the two schools of thought does not serve the same purpose. In fact, theory is not the same thing to the schools. Theory in neoclassical methodology is a "tool," a convenient fiction that is supposed to work. Theory in the Austrian methodology is an "explanation," something that makes sense of the world and makes the world more familiar to the person who possesses the theory.

The presumed equivalence between theory as a predictive tool and theory as an explanation of events has been subjected to considerable scrutiny by Coddington and has been rejected.[28] "For if explanation and prediction were structurally equivalent," writes Coddington, "predictive accuracy would be both a necessary and sufficient condition for explanatory power."[29] However, we know, for instance, that a series of historical events can be linked together in such a way as to "explain" historical episodes; however, the linking of the events may not have been developed exante to the occurrence of the events. Neoclassical theory, embodying idealized assumptions, is not intended to link actual occurrences; theory (as opposed to empirical tests) in the neoclassical paradigm is constructed largely independent of actual events. Furthermore, as Coddington argues, a prediction is mainly concerned with what will be the case, whereas an explanation is mainly concerned with the *process* by which events occur.[30] We have stressed that neoclassical theory is primarily concerned with what will actually happen and that Austrian theory is primarily concerned with the process by which outcomes occur. That is, prediction may be a sufficient but not necessary condition for an explanation.

Comparing these two views of theory can be tantamount to comparing a garden hoe with a painting of a garden; both the hoe and the painting are useful for their intended purposes. Neoclassical criticisms of Austrian theoretical economics are in ways akin to a gardener's complaint that an artist does not use a hoe to work. Similarly, Austrian criticisms of neoclaccical theoretical work are in ways akin to an artist's complaint that a gardener does not attempt to paint a picture with a hoe.

Austrians generally concede that human actions are undertaken in a variety of circumstances that exhibit different degrees of complexity. Some circumstances are extremely complex, so much so that comprehension by an outside observer of the true basis for the actions is impossible. In such circumstances, there are no true constants for testing a theory. On the other hand, other possible circumstances exhibit little complexity, and the object of action can, with reasonable accuracy, be identified. In these circumstances, constants can be agreed upon. At least, for a short period of time, the object of action remains constant and prediction can be made with some degree of accuracy.

Extreme Austrians may object to what has been said, arguing that all actions and objects of actions are extremely complex. If that were true, one might reasonably conclude that Austrians could not logically talk about "Austrian economics" or hold a meeting of Austrian economists. Agreement would never be sufficient among would-be Austrians as to who Austrian economists are and what Austrian economics is. Granted, a debate does exist over the boundaries of Austrian economics, but Austrians do congregate. Austrians are able to categorize Hayek, Menger, and von Mises as Austrian economists. There is a perceived, albeit imperfect, constant that permits rudimentary classification of Austrian and non-Austrian economics.

Austrians stress that the market is a process by which individuals adjust their actions of others. The reactions of individuals are based on information acquired in the market process and predictions founded on that acquired information. Austrians may give the impression in their theoretical discussions that all actions and reactions in the market process are taken by isolated but interacting individuals. That is, predictions are based on means and ends as evaluated by *individual* market participants — that is, entrepreneurs. In that type of world, recognition of agreed-upon constants is unnecessary. However, in most real-world markets, entrepreneurial functions are frequently carried out by *groups* of people in a bureaucratic organizational setting.[31] Predictions in those markets require groups of people to agree on what is being predicted. Within the bounds of the organizational structure, agreed-to constants are subsumed. Austrians offer no reason why the notion of constants cannot, in some cases, be extended beyond the entrepreneurial structure and cannot be adopted by the scientific community.

As Frank Knight has suggested, at times a close correspondence exists between a theoretical variable and its real-world proxy. At other times, the correspondence simply does not exist, for reasons articulated by Austrian economics.[32] Hence, predictive science is applicable to some areas of economic life but not applicable to other areas. By inference, Knight suggests that the techniques of predictive science (as opposed to abstract science) must be applied to truly *micro*economic problems — areas of human action in which events are uncomplicated and well specified and time periods are sufficiently short to preclude significant changes in people's preferences and the complex circumstances in which choices are made.

Austrians would appear to have a legitimate complaint against neoclassical economics when they attempt to apply scientific techniques to highly complex goods like "child services" and "music appreciation human capital," a subject discussed earlier in detail. Such goods do not have well defined boundaries and are not normally traded, per se, meaning that agreement on what they are is virtually impossible to achieve. There is, therefore, considerable reason to doubt that a theoretical prediction regarding child services can be subjected to an acceptable empirical test. Any empirical test of predictions regarding child services is likely to be as much a test of the appropriateness of the proxy variable as it is of any rigorously specified hypothesis. Having said that, however, Austrians cannot conclude necessarily that the price-quantity relationship for well defined goods like apples cannot be logically deduced and subjected to a limited empirical test.

Neoclassical economists argue that decisions must be made on the basis of estimated costs and benefits of alternative courses of actions. Surely, they must, for the sake of consistency, concede the possibility that some circumstances are so complex that empirical tests make no economic sense: The expected costs of adequately measuring actions or the objects of actions are too great to make empirical tests a Pareto-efficient move. Surely, neoclassical economists must concede that some levels of policy development make cost-benefit analysis uneconomical. Furthermore, if they push their methods too far, neoclassicists can become trapped in an infinite regress: If we are able to base policy decisions on estimated costs and benefits, should we not make decisions on whether to conduct empirical tests on the same basis? Should we not make the decision to estimate the costs and benefits of empirical tests on the basis of costs and benefits, and so forth? In short, it is unreasonable, if not impossible, for neoclassical economists to insist that all decisions be based on empirical work. They must concede some ground to the Austrians, who maintain that some circumstances and some levels of policy development — for example, the development of a constitution of liberty — are too complex to be submitted to adequate empirical tests and that some decisions must be made on theoretical analysis alone, which is judged in terms of validity of basic premises and internal consistency of the logic employed.

Austrians are primarily interested in discussing the broad outlines of a Lockian-style social contract that will maximize individual freedom. That is the central concern of, for example, Hayek's recent three-volume work.[33] However, much of the discussion of social contracts appears to be conducted on the assumption that the contract, once devised, will be fully operative. Any dispute subsequent to the adoption of the contract can be settled via rules laid down within the contract. There is a presumption, in other words, that rules for maximizing individual freedom and minimizing collective action can be constructed and can form an effective barrier against subsequent efforts by special interest groups to distort the substance and meaning of the adopted rules. Austrians seem to recognize the economic basis for a social contract, which has been developed in modern language by Buchanan, Nozick, and Rawls;[34] however, they seem to presume that the economic forces that necessitate a social contract in the first place are held in check by the social contract that is developed.

Neoclassicists, being pragmatic, reason that changing circumstances over time will alter the meaning of any set of constitutional rules and will necessitate some means for resolving policy conflicts that may arise within the established constitutional framework. Some workable way of settling real-world disputes must be devised; not all policy disputes can be settled in a nonconstitutional setting by reference to Rawlsian-style contractarian standard of ''justice'' and ''fairness,'' a position implied in the ''constitution of liberty.'' Economists like Stigler and Becker and lawyers like Posner, by pleading the case for strict positivist economics, are effectively suggesting a cost-benefit constitutional rule for settling real-world policy disputes. To implement such a rule, one must concede that some costs and some benefits of government or private sector actions can be measured with reasonable accuracy. The measurements that are made may have many deficiencies, but the economic question — which the person interested in solutions for real-world problems must ask — is whether a cost-benefit rule for settling issues is any more defective than consultation with legal experts on the meaning of other, less precise constitutional rules. Austrians would appear to have a reasonable criticism in suggesting that neoclassicists go too far in applying cost-benefit analysis. However, that is a criticism of degree, not of conceptual substance. Again, there seems to be room for compromise between the two schools of thought.

Concluding Comments

Neoclassicists, as represented by the Chicago school for example, and Austrians, as represented by Hayek, share a strong belief in the ''limited state.'' An overriding conclusion of this study is that their differences arise, to a significant extent, from the divergent conceptual levels at which economists in the two schools operate. Neoclassical economics largely subsumes an established government and constitutional order, imperfect and subject to change in the give-and-take of social and political events. Neoclassicists are concerned, to a large extent, with the development of reasoned (if not scientific) solutions to everyday-type problems. They are the pragmatists of the profession, willing to accept cost-benefit analysis as a guiding principle. Many Austrians in the Hayekian mold, on the other hand, are basically concerned with *the* constitutional order subsumed by neoclassicists. They attempt to make the case for limited government and free markets at a conceptual level at which the issues are so broad and nebulous that empirical analysis, of the sort required for cost-benefit studies, seems to be largely meaningless.

In the final analysis, both approaches are useful for their respective constitutional and postconstitutional levels of discussion. However, there is room for criticism. Austrians seem to have a reasonable point when they suggest that many modern-day neoclassicists forget that there are limits to their methods and that they go "too far" in applying their tools of analysis. On the other hand, the neoclassicists appear to have a reasonable criticism when they suggest that not all current social issues can be resolved by reference to broad constitutional precepts.

Notes

1. Edwin G. Dolan, ed., *The Foundations of Modern Austrian Economics* (Menlo Park, Calif.: Institute for Human Studies, 1976), p. 4.
2. Friedrich A. Hayek, *New Studies in Philosophy, Politics, Economics and the History of Ideas* (Chicago: University of Chicago Press, 1978). p. 23. Hayek cites his own "Scientism and the Study of Society," *The Counter-Revolution of Science* (Chicago: University of Chicago Press, 1952). Helmut Schoeck writes:

> Adherents of scientism — as far as the study of man is concerned — have turned the meaning of "science" (*Wissenschaft*) into the art of selective "not knowing" and "not noticing." Today's scientific bias compels students to know the worthless and keeps them from search for the knowledge of worthwhile bodies of data . . . Many of the theoretical achievements, as well as the everyday routine work of the natural sciences, depend on subjective sensory experiences, evaluations, and judgments of a kind that is strictly outlawed as "unscientific" or "unscholarly" in the official social sciences of today.

3. Lionel Robbins, *The Nature and Significance of Economic Science,* 2d ed. (New York: Macmillan, 1973), p. 16.
4. Philip H. Wicksteed, *The Common Sense of Political Economy,* vols. 1 and 2 (New York: Augustus M. Kelley, 1967), pp. 159–61, 776–80; Helmut Schoeck and James W. Wiggins, eds., "Introduction," *Scientism and Values* (Princeton, N.J.: D. Van Nostrand, 1960), p. xxi.
5. Milton Friedman, *Essays in Positive Economics* (Chicago: University of Chicago Press, 1953), pp. 3–43.
6. Von Mises has written,

> Man acts because he is dissatisfied with the state of affairs as it prevails in the absence of his intervention. Man acts because he lacks the power to render conditions fully satisfactory and must resort to appropriate means in order to render them less unsatisfactory. [Ludwig von Mises, *The Ultimate Foundations of Economic Science* (Menlo Park, Calif.: Institute for Human Studies, 1976), pp. 2–3]

7. Dolan, *The Foundations,* p. 5.
8. Ludwig von Mises, *Human Action: A Treatise on Economics* (New Haven, Ct.: Yale University Press, 1963), pp. 55–56.
9. Murry H. Rothbard, "Praxeology: The Methodology of Austrian Economics," in Dolan, *The Foundations,* p. 19.
10. Ibid., p. 21.
11. Hayek, *New Studies,* p. 28.
12. "The only relevant test of the validity of a hypothesis" writes Friedman, "is comparison of its predictions with experience. The hypothesis is rejected if its predictions are contradicted ('frequently' or more often than predictions from an alternative hypothesis); it is accepted if its predictions are not

contradicted; great confidence is attached to it if it has survived many opportunities for contradiction.'' (*Essays*, pp. 8–9)

   13. Ibid., p. 7.

   14. Ibid.

   15. Ibid., pp. 10–11.

   16. George J. Stigler, *The Citizen and the State: Essays on Regulation* (Chicago: University of Chicago Press, 1975), pp. 4–5.

   17. Ibid., p. 56.

   18. Some Austrians go so far as to suggest that one cannot even predict and test empirically the statement that the higher the price, the lower the quantity of apples purchased or that the higher the tariff imposed upon imported textiles, the lower the quantity of textiles imported. They argue: We cannot measure the ''apples'' and ''textiles;'' therefore, we have no way of saying ''factually'' whether or not the statement is true. We can, on the other hand, logically deduce that people, interested in pursuing their own interest, will buy less of a ''good'' that is wanted when its price rises, ceteris paribus. In such a statement the ''good'' is left undefined. The ''rightness'' or ''wrongness'' of the statement is determined by the validity of the premises on which the statement is determined and the internal consistency of the logic that leads to the statement.

   19. See Friedman, *Essays*, p. 7; and Alfred Marshall, ''The Present Position of Economics,'' *Memorial of Alfred Marshall*, ed. A.C. Pigou (*London: Macmillan* and Company, 1925).

   20. Kenneth E. Boulding, *Economics as a Science* (New York: McGraw-Hill, 1970), p. 2.

   21. Alan Coddington, ''Positive Economics'' *Canadian Journal of Economics,* February 1972, p. 8. Coddington cites Alfred Marshall (*Principles of Economics* [London: n.d., 1972], pp. 6 and 638.)

   22. Ibid., p. 4.

   23. See, for example of ways the terms are used, Friedrich A. Hayek, ''Degrees of Explanation'' and ''The Theory of Complex Phenomena,'' *Studies in Philosophy, Politics, and Economics* (Chicago: University of Chicago Press, 1967), pp. 3–42.

   24. Ibid., p. 17. Hayek writes:

> The service of a theory which does not tell us what particular events to expect at a definite moment, but only what kinds of events we are to expect within a certain range, or on complexities of certain type, would perhaps be better described by the term orientation than by speaking of prediction. Although such a theory does not tell us precisely what to expect, it will still make the world around us a more familiar world in which we can move with greater confidence, that we shall not be disappointed because we can at least exclude certain eventualities. It makes it a more orderly world in which the events make sense because we can at least say in general terms how they hang together or are able to form a coherent picture of them. Though we are not in a position to specify precisely what to expect, or even to list the possibilities, each observed pattern has meaning in the sense that it limits the possibilities of what else may occur. [p. 18]

   25. Ibid., p. 16.

   26. Ibid., p. 35.

   27. Friedrich A. Hayek, *The Road to Serfdom* (Chicago: University of Chicago Press, 1942).

   28. Coddington, ''Posivitive Economics.''

   29. Ibid., p. 5.

   30. Ibid.

   31. Kirzner recognizes the potential inconsistency within Austrian Economics between the presumed unpredictability of knowledge and the presumed learning that occurs within the market process. Israel M. Kirzner, ''On the Method of Austrian Economics,'' in Dolan, *The Foundations,* pp. 48–50.

   32. These are points made frequently by Knight in his class lectures and related to the author by James Buchanan, a student of Knight.

33.   Friedrich A. Hayek, *Law, Legislation and Liberty,* vols. I–III (Chicago: University of Chicago Press, 1973, 1976, and 1979).

34.   James M. Buchanan, *The Limits of Liberty: Between Anarchy and Leviathan* (Chicago: University of Chicago Press, 1975); Robert Nozick, *Anarchy, State, and Utopia* (New York: Basic Books, 1974); and John Rawls, *A Theory of Justice* (Cambridge, Mass.: Harvard University Press, 1971).

5 THE NECESSARY NORMATIVE CONTEXT OF POSITIVE ECONOMICS

"'Reality'' is what we take to be true. What we take to be true is what we believe. What we believe is based upon our perceptions. What we perceive depends on what we look for. What we look for depends upon what we think. What we think depends upon what we perceive. What we believe determines what we take to be true. What we take to be true is our reality.

— Gary Zukav
The Dancing of the Wu Li Masters

In recent decades economists have in many significant ways refined and made more sophisticated their theoretical and empirical techniques. Concomitantly, economics has gained considerable acceptance in the media and government circles as an important basis for the development of politically acceptable, if not efficient, public policies.[1] Proponents of social reform actively seek the counsel of economists in the development of their reform packages. These proponents (and their opposition) understand that the success or failure of proposed policy changes often, but not always, hinges on the findings of scholarly economic studies.

The modern prominence of economics in the development of public policy has been founded upon the generally accepted presumption that the investigatory techniques used successfully for centuries in the physical sciences are readily and with only minor modification applicable to the study of human interaction in the marketplace and elsewhere. Accordingly, many economists and policymakers firmly believe that economics provides a largely (if not totally) mechanical, nonnormative, impersonal, and independent means of seeking social improvement. A presumption commonly made is that the goals of economics as a course of study

This is a revised version of an article that appeared in the September 1981 issue of the *Journal of Economic Issues*. Reprinted by special permission of the copyright holder, the Association for Evolutionary Economics.

can be pursued with the same objective detachment used by the chemist probing the molecular structure of sodium or the physicist examining the "makeup" of light.

A limited but growing number of economists and critics from adjoining disciplines have begun to have second thoughts concerning the "scientific capacity" of economics — that is, the ability of the discipline to deliver the positive, objective perspective so often claimed as its hallmark.[2] Austrian economists have grave reservations about accepting the "scientific" work (ingraciously tagged "scientism") of much modern economics.[3] As Kenneth Boulding wrote a number of years ago, in spite of economics' academic origins in moral philosophy, modern economists have been taught to believe that they actually can escape the "swaddling clothes of moral judgment," whereas "the propositions of science are no more immaculately conceived than the preferences of individuals."[4] More recently, in an admittedly unscientific but provocative article, Warren Samuels addresses an issue that may, perhaps, be viewed as a contradiction in terms by most positive economists, the normative dimensions of positive economics.[5] In raising that issue once again and ascribing normative elements to presumably "hard," "fixed," and "scientific" conclusions from the neoclassical paradigm (such as the frequently touted statement that free trade maximizes output and improves welfare), Samuels casts doubt over the social worthiness of much economic analysis. He suggests that economics is — if not totally, then to a significant extent — a "system of beliefs" and that many uses of economics "may represent only the clothing of normativism with the garments of science, confusing the social role of the analyst with that of the moral teacher, priest, and advocate."[6]

Implied in Samuels' analysis of his survey results is the question of whether or not the roles of the "analyst" and "moral teacher" can, in fact or even conceptually, be disentangled in matters of social policy. Must not an analyst-qua-economist *be* a moral philosopher (in much the same spirit that Adam Smith was)? Can "positive economics" avoid being guided, molded, and ordered by convictions of what people and society should be? And, finally, does not the virtual denial of a moral foundation for economics and the treatment of economic analysis as though it were the work of technicians (who, if the technology were available, could be replaced by mechanical robots) detract from the social significance of what economists claim to be saying?

These are the types of questions addressed in this chapter. To gain a partial understanding of these perplexing issues, we first reflect on how economics is viewed as a science and then consider where and to what extent scientific economics can be compared to, say, physics. The general conclusion drawn is that economics must have a didactic intent (in ways not explicitly recognized by Boulding and Samuels) and that much policy disagreement among economists and between economists and analysts from other disciplines surfaces not only from differences in the perception of policy consequences (a point stressed by Friedman),[7] but from differences in the didactic context from which positive conclusions *must* be drawn.

Economics as a Science

Robert Mundell opens the preface to one of his books with the blunt claim that "Economics is *the* science of choice" (emphasis added), echoing the sentiments of many other economists.[8] Milton Friedman goes to considerable trouble in his seminal methodological article to convince skeptics that economics not only *does* but *should* and *must* emulate the investigatory approach of the hard sciences. Writing about the distinction between normative and positive economics, Friedman concludes, "In short, positive economics is, or can be, an 'objective' science, in precisely the same sense as any of the physical sciences."[9]

As a science, economics is thought to unravel in a systematic way the mysteries of much of the social world that surrounds us. The view commonly adopted by economists is that their work deals not so much with man's self-imposed illusions about the "real world," but with the real world itself. Any mental illusions (or constructs) employed in models of the real-world economy, for example, are used as convenient fictions for ultimately grasping the handle of what actually constitutes the "real world." Models are thought to "explain" the real world insofar (and only insofar) as they organize "things," "events," and "actions" into patterns or relationships and predict events and actions external to the economist-observer-analyst.[10] Those have been the lessons grasped from previous chapters.

Logical positivists recognize that their theories and empirical models are illusory in the sense that they are figments of the fertile, albeit scientific, imaginations, ordered more by the needs and limitations of the mind to "comprehend" the external, objective world than by the needs and limitations (if there are any) of the external, objective world that is the object of the analysis. As noted in chapter 4, neoclassical theories and models of the real world are intended to provide understanding in the form of predictions — to accomplish a specific task, much as a hoe is intended to be used in gardening — and are not themselves intended to *be* the real world. However, given the nature of such "understanding," the distinction between the means of understanding (that is, theories and models) and the real world itself can easily (and "understandably") become blurred and, perhaps, made irrelevant in discussions of what economists do. Analysis, therefore, often proceeds *as if* both theories and the object of the theories are one and the same. So it is that many economists view the law of demand not as a mental device for ordering and comprehending human behavior (constructed within the context of the limitations of the mind to understand), but as a law — perhaps natural in origin — that they have discovered or, should we say, uncovered.

The scientific perspective adopted by modern economics is, contrary to the perception of many economists, founded upon a very special view of nature, including human action and interaction. Outside of the context of people's efforts to "understand" natural processes, all that is a part of nature can be viewed as a profusion of outcomes that just occur and continue to occur. In nature, by itself and unobserved by the human mind, there are, as physicists sometimes note, no correlations.[11] Or, at least, that is one way of looking at nature — a way, we might add, which the scientific perspective of nature explicitly rejects. Understanding necessitates, or so it seems, a willingness on the part of the observer-analyst to take the position that order can be found in apparent chaos. The drive for understanding suggests that the scientific mind either needs or wants to derive the order that it, itself, effectively creates (which is a way of saying "discovers" within nature or within the mind that is, of course, a part of nature). Hence, in this regard science may be viewed as much as a commentary on the needs and limits of the subjective consciousness as it is an explanation of the external objective world.

The very goal of science, and logical positivism, necessitates an underlying vision of the world and universe and, if science is to be pursued, a commitment to that vision. It is very hard to see how such a commitment can be anything other than normative, ethically founded in much the same spirit that people believe in God and in the sense that there is some choice in the matter of world views. If there is no choice in the matter of world visions, then understanding appears to lose its commonsense interpretation, and science becomes nothing more or less than part and parcel of the mindless profusion of natural events, tantamount to self-delusion, not understanding.

The very concept of "understanding" implies the acceptance of an ethical position. On one level "understanding" is very subjective and the nature of "science" is judged individually. On quite another level "science" is an activity pursued by a community for the *purposes* of (implicitly or explicitly stated by) the community. And in the scientific process, as a communal endeavor, is an elaborate ethical structure of what science *should* be. Kenneth Boulding notes the "scientific subculture" places an extraordinarily high value "on veracity, on curiosity, on measurement, on quantification, on careful observation and experimentation, and on objectivity," to which he adds: "The question as to exactly what values and ethical propositions are essential to the scientific subculture may be in some dispute. The fact that there are values cannot be disputed."[12]

The normative content of any science, especially social science, is encountered directly in efforts to verify prediction of theory. Even in the natural sciences the process of verification is not — cannot be — completely neutral. Determination of the coincidence of conclusions from theory with reality is beset with measurement problems. The inability to measure events that occur in a chainlike procession before a volcano erupts may be as much at the heart of the inability to predict eruptions as is the lack of a theory of volcano eruptions. As David Maxwell has pointed out to me, "In the 'soft' sciences (including economics), determination of coincidence between conclusions and reality is an arduous task akin to measuring a table with an elastic ruler. There is no neutral way of determining such coincidence. Praxeologists maintain that the attempt is useless since the constructs that we must use are those provided by theory and are incapable of accepting information not consistent with the theory. So, why bother?''[13]

Chicago-type economists operate as if problems of verification do not exist and simply presume that the matching of conclusions (that is, predictions) with measured reality is a neutral step. If there are problems of ''matching,'' one must rightfully wonder whether the empirical test is a test of the validity of the theory or a test of the extent to which the measured world corresponds with the theoretical constructs. If the process of verification cannot be defended on any grounds other than its ability to predict, then we are left to wonder whether the process of science is not empty, since we do not know what is the subject of the test. The very fact that Chicago-type economists commit themselves to empirical verification must have intrinsic, value-laden judgments about ''tests.'' Otherwise, there would be nothing to test.

Einstein, Friedman, and Economics

Albert Einstein, whom we study in considerable detail in chapter 6, is the quintessential physicist of the twentieth century and, perhaps, of all time. Almost single-handedly, he restructured man's concept of the universe. However, his theoretical accomplishments, mainly in the form of his theories of special and general relativity, stemmed not so much from superior mathematical abilities (he was not a great mathematician and often fretted about not having the mathematical skills he needed), nor from associations with the great physicists of his time (he developed his special theory of relativity while employed as an inspector third-class in a Swiss patent office), nor from special research findings that were exclusively available to him (he was not an empiricist). Rather, he was able to accomplish a great deal because of an abiding, almost religious conviction in the transcending order and unity of the universe. His approach to science is summed up in these autobiographical comments on how the theories of special and general relativity came to him:

> Out yonder there was this huge world, which exists independently of us human beings and which stands before us like a great, ethical riddle, at least partially accessible to our inspection and thinking. The contemplation of this world beckoned like a liberation, and I soon noticed that many a man whom I had learned to esteem and admire had found inner freedom and security in devoted occupation with it. The mental grasp of this extrapersonal world within the frame of the given possibilities swam as highest aim half consciously and half unconsciously before my mind's eye.[14]

In 1901, after he had grasped the essentials of special relativity, Einstein wrote to his friend Michael Grossmann, ''It is a magnificent feeling to recognize the unity of a complex of phenomena which appear to be things quite apart from the direct visible truth.''[15] And on another occasion he wrote, ''This deep intuitive conviction of the existence of a higher power of thought which manifests itself in the inscrutable universe represents the content of my definition of God.''[16] Only someone who had Einstein's ''thirst for unity'' could have possibly conceived of the intermingling of time, space, mass, and energy in the way he did. Because of this ''thirst,'' Einstein rejected Neil Bohr's quantum mechanics as anything other than a stopgap explanation of the way the world works. Einstein's concern was that Bohr's theory can only predict the ''probable'' position of the electron in its orbit within the atom; it cannot predict the exact movement of each electron.

Einstein was convinced that ''God does not play dice with the universe'' nor send electrons shooting randomly around the nucleus of the atom. In his search for a unified field theory — and thereby a general conception of ''what is'' — during the last thirty or so years of his life, Einstein was guided by the ''belief'' that there are universal laws that can explain each and every event within the microcosm as well as the macrocosm. As with his theory of general relativity, the perspective of the observer must not alter the governing laws, within either the atomic or planetary systems. His view of universal determinism ultimately led him to what many neoclassical-Chicago-style economists would consider an inept analysis of social events and the efficiency *and* morality of unplanned, free market economies.[17] In his view, capitalism is immoral because it is *dis*harmonizing; that is, it works against the transcending order of nature.[18]

Positive economics, as represented, for example, by the methodological positions and applied theories of Milton Friedman, Gary Becker, and George Stigler, is very similar to (but not identical with) the type of science done by Einstein and most modern physicists. Economists implicitly adopt the ethical structure (described above by Boulding) of how science should be conducted; they may add, however, that the values of veracity, curiosity, objectivity, and so forth tend to be held in check by professional competition for ''fame and fortune.'' Both economists and physicists tend to accept empirical probability as the main criterion for judging a theory's ''usefulness'' and ''importance.'' Both groups place a great deal of stock in theoretical simplicity, although for somewhat different reasons. Einstein, for example, cherished theoretical simplicity because he believed it to be a form of beauty and a more effective expression of the ''true mind of God'' (if there were a God).[19] Friedman, Becker, and Stigler, on the other hand, look upon theoretical simplicity as a means of reducing the cost of analysis.[20] Friedman writes that ''the only relevant test of the *validity* of a hypothesis is comparison of its predictions with experience,'' but then qualifies his stance:

> Here there are two important external standards of comparison. One is the accuracy achievable by alternative theory with which this theory is being compared and which is equally acceptable on all other grounds. The other arises when there exists a theory that is

known to yield better predictions but only at greater costs. The gains from greater accuracy, which depend on the purpose in mind, must then be balanced against the cost of achieving it.[21]

If normative considerations have no influence on positive economics, one can only wonder about the origins of the preference structure that enables the positive analyst to strike the "proper balance" between theoretical simplicity and predictability.

The objective function of positive economics and the physical sciences is actually quite complex. Both often stress that the realism of underlying assumptions is more or less irrelevant in evaluating a theory, a position that tends to place a great deal of weight on predictive accuracy. Physicists must take such a position since, in areas like quantum mechanics, theorists do not know the nature of the "substances" (if there are any) with which they are dealing. All they can do is talk in terms of concepts like electrons, protons, and quarks (called "charm," "beauty," "truth," and others not yet discovered) and *measure* them as they come into contact with measuring devices. Economists, on the other hand, deal with human values, which are about as elusive as quarks, to specify objectively. However, as Austrian economists repeatedly point out, economists have at their disposal one tool of analysis physicists do not have — introspection: Economists can assess, within limits, the validity of assumptions by simply asking if the assumptions match very well with their own and others' experiences.[22] Physicists cannot do the same with regard to quarks. Friedman argues forcefully that "the relevant question to ask about the 'assumptions' of a theory is not whether they are descriptively 'realistic,' for they never are, but whether they are sufficiently good approximations for the purpose in hand."[23]

Economists like Friedman and physicists like Einstein differ significantly over what "predictive theory" implies or reveals. To Friedman, a highly predictive theory is a useful "instrument." There is no necessary connection between the way an economist formulates a prediction and what the laws of the universe are: The theory is a tool for making predictions, nothing more nor less. Einstein, on the other hand, looked upon theoretical statements as more than a tool — as human expressions of the order that exists in the universe or as statements of the "mind of God" (a phrase Einstein used without the usual religious connotation).

Logical positivists often give the impression that predictions are all that matter in theory construction. However, if given the choice between two equally predictive theories, one of which is considered "more realistic" than the other, would we not expect positive economists like Friedman to adopt the more realistic theory? Should we not expect those who readily employ convex indifference curves in much of their theoretical analysis to consider trade-offs between the "descriptive realism" and the "predictive power" of theories? Granted, the predictive power of theories may appear to be a matter of "hard and cold" facts, but that is not always and everywhere the case. Both "descriptive realism" and "predictive power" are, at least at times, partially subjective in origin, dependent upon agreement for their meaning.[24]

Even if such a line of argument can be dismissed as an overly aggressive interpretation and extension of "normal positivist" philosophy, it is reasonably clear that positivists do include in their objective function such things as "fruitfulness," "logical completeness," and "consistency" as well as "simplicity."[25] Given their emphasis on "trade-offs" in all other aspects of life, it would appear that positivist economists would have to agree that there must be some normative basis for balancing the several objectives of their type of science.

The Catch-22 in Science

Several of the normative dimensions of positive economics have been noted by other authors. Samuels asks, "What are the normative elements which constrain and make conditional the positive content of the proposition [free trade will maximize the value of output]?" He concludes,

> (1) The choice of maximization of value of output as the presumed objective of the economic system is normative. (2) There is no one maximum value of output. It varies, and noncomparably, with price structure and output definitions. These latter and the weighting of output by utility function are dependent upon and generally specific to rights and are normative. The price structure is a function of and specific to the income, wealth, and power structures of society and are normative . . . (3) Maximization of the value of output involves index number problems whose solutions are normative. (4) The income, wealth, and power consequences of value of output maximization are normative. (5) Maximization of the value of output is a deductive implication which is nonoperational, nontestable, and nonrefutable.[26]

Paul Heyne adds other normative elements: The choice of social problems to be addressed by economists is largely normative. The consequences of social investigation by economists are, thereby, normative in nature since the attention given to specific social issues, to the exclusion of others deemed "less pressing," means segments of society will be affected by what is presumed to be detached and neutral theory.[27]

Although these considerations are important, the central theme of this chapter is that the normative content of economics necessarily begins at a fundamental level — at the point at which economics is presumed to be a "science" — not so much with the particular assumptions of economic analysis and the particular direction the analysis takes, the focus of Samuels, Heyne, and others.

Heyne closes his outstanding introductory economics text with words that must be etched on the forehead of every economist who presumes to be a scientist: "But some point of view is indispensable to any inquiry, in the physical sciences as well as in the social sciences. A completely open mind is a completely empty mind, and empty minds learn nothing.''[28] There is no argument with such a position. Indeed, embedded in such a scientific perspective is a kind of "scientific catch-22." Scientists attempt to learn about the world in which they live. However, they must have some means, some method, of wading through — of selecting and interpreting — the buzzing confusion of information they confront on a daily basis. The development of a model of the world means that some information will be the subject of study while other information will be ignored to one degree or another; therefore, an interpretation of the "buzzing confusion" is, in a sense, predetermined.

The "catch" surfaces when we ask, How does one extend one's learning when the mind must be "closed"? When we have learned nothing — and face the "buzzing confusion" as, figuratively and literally speaking, "scientific virgins" — how do we learn anything? Where do we start — that is, obtain that first inspiration to inquire, to model, and to learn? Once we have our model of the world, how do we guard against closing the mind so completely that learning is choked off, that no new theories of relativity — no new intuitive insights — are developed? As Gary Zukav suggests in the chapter-opening quotation, Is not what we believe and perceive to be true inextricably bound up in our concept of reality, in the type of science we do? These are the types of questions that must be faced by positive economists who go to great lengths to deny any normative basis for what they do.

Needless to say, a "starting point" must be a *starting point,* determined by many factors — some genetic, some historical, some scientific, but also some normative, a kind of artistic, poetic vision of what the world *should* be — all of which are antecedent to and guide the *selection* of a priori assumptions.[29] Similarly, the progression of science in statements of "what is" must be guided in principle by principles that transcend the process of narrowly focused "research programmes," a phrase original with I. Lakatos and applied by Brian Loasby.[30]

The Individual, Freedom, and Science

In a scathing attack on much modern economics, particularly neoclassical-positive economics, Murray Rothbard writes:

> Scientism is the profoundly unscientific attempt to transfer uncritically the methodology of the physical sciences to the study of human action. Both fields of inquiry must, it is true, be studied by the use of reason — the mind's identification of reality. But then it becomes critically important, in reason, not to neglect the critical attribute of human action: that, alone in nature, human beings possess a rational consciousness. Stones, molecules, planets cannot *choose* their courses, their behavior is strictly and mechanically determined for them. Only human beings possess free will and consciousness.[31]

Interestingly, much neoclassical economics is founded upon the very proposition Rothbard hails as the distinguishing feature of the human experience: Human beings, as individuals, act consciously and purposefully. The individual, as a choosing agent, is critical to consumer preference theory, a building block on the way to a theory of markets and a logic of collective action within nonmarket social arrangements. As suggested by Rothbard (as well as by the works of Hayek and von Mises cited above), the role of the "acting individual" is pivotal to Austrian economics, or praxeology. And contrary to Rothbard, the concept of the acting individual is central to neoclassical-positive economics: It leads to a theory of social interaction that is very "useful" — that is, often highly fruitful in terms of correct predictions. The instrumental use of the "acting individual" in positive economics is not at issue here. What is at issue is whether or not the concept of the acting individual is normative, a statement, albeit implicit, about the way the world *ought* to be viewed and a context within which positive positions of "what is" can be developed.

To the strict logical positivist, the individual is a convenient theoretical construct. His identity is described by a set of assumptions regarding the contents of his objective function and the constraints he faces. He is neither more nor less than the mathematical symbols that represent him. However, if that is all the individual is, we must wonder why the positivist persists in using him as a construct. There are other alternative constructs: "Group," "community," and "society" are three possible and very good candidates. From the valueless view of positivism, there is no necessary reason for concentrating on the individual as opposed to "society." The individual may *appear* to be an easily identifiable social entity, and that is reason enough to start a theory somewhat arbitrarily with the individual as the focal point. However, the individual is part and parcel of a social process — a society — and as Frank Knight stressed, the individual is as dependent upon the social context in which he exists for his own identity as he is upon himself.[32] The individual has values, but those values are perhaps as much a product of his social context as they are of the power of the individual to create them. The relevant unit of social analysis *can be* and *is* different for different groups of social analysts, with differing emphasis on the independence of the individual from the group versus the dependence of the individual upon the group and differing views of the consequences of social policies.

Economists who start their analysis with emphasis on the conceptual identity of the individual (almost) invariably end with very definite conclusions relating to the effectiveness of the market in fulfilling "individual values" (where third-party effects and monopoly power are absent). However, it must be emphasized again and again that all of this analysis is dependent upon the implicit normative assumption that the individual human being is "important" in the sense that his values count.

Often, the attention given to the individual has been vaguely justified on the grounds that human beings are distinctive from their counterparts in the rest of nature — they think and have a rational capacity. Growing evidence suggests many other animals — from rodents to birds to dolphins — and even some plants have a rational capacity, a consciousness, and the ability to respond to emotional stimuli, like hostility and affection. Admittedly, the evidence is, at this point, somewhat primitive and unconvincing. Nevertheless, it challenges usual presumptions about the scientific uniqueness of the human experience and causes us to recognize that concentration on individual human beings, and their values, has more of a theological than scientific basis.

Clearly, if all values of all living things are given equal status in economic theory, nothing can be said about the Pareto efficiency of market solutions. Each exchange of a pound of beef or a squash may be beneficial to the people engaging in the transactions but harmful to the steer or the squash plant. Of course, positive economists do not trace out those "third-party effects" — for good normative reasons. Because of religious beliefs, personal preferences, and/or what is perceived as truth in the natural ordering of things, people count as individual in economic analysis, whereas plants and nonhuman animals do not. Again, as Zukav suggests at the start of this chapter, reality and perceived truth become inextricably fused in social theory.

Einstein, who perceived social unity as critically important and society as the relevant theoretical construct, despaired of capitalism's usefulness mainly because he believed capitalism tends to aggravate "egotistic values" and suppress natural "community values" and "community unity." More will be said on Einstein's views in chapter 6. The important point is that where the whole of society is the relevant theoretical construct — the total focus of analysis — the concepts of cost (in terms of *individual* options foregone) and efficiency lose their conventional economic meaning. When viewed from the different perspectives of the individualist and the collectivist, conclusions regarding the consequences of public policies are largely noncomparable. Granted, a strict positivist may retort that use of the individual yields highly predictive theories, but this point of view is often espoused by positivists who have never attempted to undertake research based on the "community" or "society" and on "social values" as opposed to "individual values."

Further, when the relevant unit of analysis in different theories is not the same, what "comparative predictive accuracy" means is not clear. The predictions are largely directed at different things, different goals, none of which can be accurately specified. The problem individualists and collectivists confront when they debate the merits of public policies is that they are effectively talking at cross-purposes, inspired by different normative foundations.

The purpose of these comments is not to denigrate positivism and its advocates; rather, it is to stress that the allegiance positivists (especially from the Chicago school) place on the individual has more than instrumental worth. The allegiance is a declaration of the moral merit of the individual as a social entity. It is a commitment to the *value* of individual differences within the context of the whole of society and of individual freedom in the face of the imposition of other people's preferences through expressions, democratic or otherwise, of the "collective will." Hence, the concept of "Pareto-efficient trades," as Samuels found in his survey, makes sense — is a statement of moral improvement and carries moral force — only as long as the moral worth of the individual is understood, declared, and appreciated. Otherwise, Pareto efficiency is just so much talk in theoretical gamesmanship.

Ascribing normative foundations to economics does not rob the analysis of a market economy of its positive content, nor does it detract from the social contribution of economists. As James Buchanan has noted, the social role of the economist-qua-philosopher can be quite didactic: "the instruction of the masses in the necessary value of a free society (in the individualistic sense)."[33] At the same time, his social function can, within that normative context and within the limited applicability of science to social events,[34] include extensive and exhaustive statements of what *will* emerge in a free society and what *will be* the consequence of various public policies. The professional and public esteem enjoyed by economists like Friedman, Stigler, and Samuelson is partially attributable to their insistence on strict adherence to scientific standards for social investigation — but there is more to it than that. People sense in them a commitment to some higher goal — some transcending normative purpose — that guides and shapes their research and their social commentary. Technicians who take a given set of assumptions, follow the rules of logic, manipulate complicated mathematical formulas to find the first- and second-order conditions, and empirically test rigidly specified hypotheses are important to the development of any science, *but they are also plentiful.* The scarce commodity is the true scientist who is able to combine the role of technician and technical competence with the role of visionary and a sense of ultimate purpose. That is the combination that Adam Smith and his modern followers exhibit.

Concluding Comments

In an article cited earlier, Kenneth Boulding notes that one of the most absurd bits of ancient Latin wisdom is *de gustibus non disputandum* because "we spend most of our lives disputing about tastes."[35] By stressing the techniques of positive economics, economists have grown to believe that they have risen above disputes over tastes and have found a means of providing guidance for policymakers, purified of any normative position of the investigator. On the contrary, the social importance of economic analysis is enhanced when the necessary normative context of economic analysis is openly admitted. Social scientists, as distinguished from research technicians, must not only test the relevance of their science, but must also be prepared to test in open forum the normative context within which their science is conducted. The importance of the recent work of people like John Rawls, Friedrich Hayek, James Buchanan, and Robert Nozick is that moral philosophy has been squarely reintroduced to the debate over the appropriate role of government.[36] These analysts have shown that there are legitimate and very productive conceptual ways of "disputing tastes." To appreciate the worth of their own research, economists must understand the nature of that debate over the justice (or "fairness") of the social setting in which the framework of an economic system (and government) is constructed and within which Pareto efficiency has meaning. In the long run such concerns are probably all that really matter.

Notes

1. Indeed, economists like George Stigler argue that economics has reached the threshold of its disciplinary "golden age" as a result of the reliance economists place on their professional calculations of the gains and costs of proposed social reform, the hallmark of much economic analysis. (George J. Stigler, "The Economist and the State," *The Citizen and the State: Essays on Regulation* [Chicago: University of Chicago Press, 1975], pp. 38–60).

2. See, for example, Friedrich A. Hayek, "The Economy, Science, and Politics," *Studies in Philosophy, Politics and Economics* (Chicago: University of Chicago Press, 1967), pp. 259–69; and various essays in Helmut Schoeck and James W. Wiggins, eds., *Scientism and Values* (New York: D. Van Nostrand, 1960); and Warren J. Samuels, ed., *The Chicago School of Political Economy* (East Lansing: University of Michigan Press, 1977).

3. For a more detailed comparison of several of the methodological positions of neoclassicists and Austrians, see chapter 4. Most Austrians still recognize a proper, albeit limited, role for science in economic inquiry. The nub of the dispute between the neoclassicists and the Austrians is the question of how much of human social organization can be understood with the full range of "scientific techniques" that presumably distinguish physics from, say, art, not whether or not social inquiry is useless (although some Austrians appear to believe it is). Austrians are principally concerned with the efforts of neoclassical economists to quantify and empirically test conclusions drawn from economic models.

4. Kenneth E. Boulding, "Economics as a Moral Science," *Economics as a Science* (New York: McGraw-Hill, 1970), pp. 117, 119.

5. Warren J. Samuels, "Economics as a Science and Its Relation to Policy: The Example of Free Trade," *Journal of Economic Issues,* March 1980, pp. 163–85.

6. Ibid., p. 180.

7. Milton Friedman, "The Methodology of Positive Economics," *Essays in Positive Economics* (Chicago: University of Chicago Press, 1953), pp. 3–43.

8. Robert Mundell, *Man and Economics* (New York: McGraw-Hill, 1968), p. ii. James Buchanan questions the internal consistency of such a statement in "Is Economics a Science of Choice?" (*Roads to Freedom,* Erich Stressler, ed. [London: Routledge and Kegan Paul, 1969], pp. 47–64); however, it should be noted that Buchanan's central purpose was with whether choice can be the foundation of predictions and, therefore, any *scientific* inquiry.

9.   Friedman, "The Methodology of Positive Economics," p. 4.

10.   Edwin Dolan makes a useful distinction between "events" and "actions." An event is something that just happens in the course of nature, such as a tree falling in the forest. "An action, in contrast," writes Dolan, "is something that happens as a result of purposeful intervention in the 'natural' course of things" (Edwin G. Dolan, "Austrian Economics as Extraordinary Science," *The Foundations of Modern Austrians Economics* [Kansas City, Mo.: Sheed and Ward, 1976], p. 5).

11.   As physicist Henry Stapp writes, "A long-range correlation between observables has the interesting property that the equation of motion which governs the propagation of this effect is precisely the equation of motion of a freely moving particle" ("S-Matrix Interpretation of Quantum Theory," *Physical Review,* December 3, 1971). Gary Zukav, who is quoted at the chapter opening, adds, "Things are not 'correlated' in nature. In nature, things are as they are. Period. 'Correlation' is a concept which *we* use to describe connections which *we* perceive. There is no word, 'correlation,' apart from people. There is no concept, 'correlation,' apart from people. This is because only people use words and concepts" (*The Dancing of the Wu Li Masters: An Overview of the New Physics* [New York: Bantam Books, 1980], p. 71).

12.   Boulding, "Economics as a Moral Science," pp. 119–20.

13.   W. David Maxwell, personal correspondence (October 1, 1981).

14.   Albert Einstein, "Autobiographical Notes," *Albert Einstein: Philosopher-Scientist,* Paul Arthur Schilpp, ed. (LaSalle, Ill.: Open Court Publishing, [The Library of Living Philosophers], 1949), p. 5.

15.   As quoted in Ronald W. Clark, *Einstein: The Life and Times* (New York: Avon Books, 1971), p. 77.

16.   As quoted in Boris Kuznetsov, "Einstein, Science and Culture," in A.P. French, ed., *Einstein: A Centenary Volume* (Cambridge, Mass.: Harvard University Press, 1979), p. 168.

17.   For more details on Einstein's economics and social commentary, see chapter 6. For now it should be noted that Einstein accepted and articulated a highly Marxian view of the market economy, incorporating a rudimentary theory of labor exploitation and surplus value, a labor theory of value, a dialectic conflict between the growth in technology and social institutions, a theory of capitalistic imperialism, and a theory of the ultimate collapse of capitalism. With regard to Einstein's views on the causes of the Great Depression, see chapter 6.

18.   Ibid. See also Albert Einstein, "Why Socialism?" *Out of My Later Years* (Secaucus, N.J.: The Citadel Press, 1956), pp. 123–31.

19.   Einstein writes, "A theory is the more impressive the greater the simplicity of its premises is, the more different kinds of things it relates, and the more extended is its area of applicability" ("Autobiographical Notes," p. 33), which is the type of statement that must be juxtaposed with, "I want my peace. I want to know how God created this world. I am not interested in this or that phenomena in the spectrum of this or that element. I want to know His thoughts, the rest are details" (as quoted in Clark, *Einstein,* p. 37). He also lived by the creed that theory should be made as simple as possible, but not simpler.

20.   Friedman makes almost the exact same point Einstein makes in the first part of note 19: "A theory is 'simpler' the less the initial knowledge needed to make a prediction within a given field of phenomena; it is more 'fruitful' the more precise the resulting prediction, the wider the area within which the theory yields predictions, and the more additional lines for further research it suggests" ("The Methodology of Positive Economics," p. 10).

21.   Friedman, "The Methodology of Positive Economics," pp. 8–9, 17. See also Gary Becker, *The Economic Approach to Human Behavior* (Chicago: University of Chicago Press, 1976), chapter 1; and George J. Stigler and Gary S. Becker, "De Gustibus Non Est Disputandum," *American Economic Review,* March 1977, pp. 76–90.

22.   See, for example, Ludwin von Mises, *The Ultimate Foundation of Economics* (Kansas City,

Mo.: Sheed Andrews and McNeel, 1976 [original 1962]), especially chapter 2. Von Mises writes as follows: "The starting point of all praxeological thinking is not arbitrarily chosen axioms, but a self-evident proposition, fully, clearly and necessarily present in every human mind . . . The starting point of praxeology is a self-evident truth, the cognition of action, that is, the cognition of the fact that there is such a thing as consciously aiming at ends" (pp. 4–6).

23. Friedman, "The Methodology of Positive Economics," p. 15.

24. Clearly, with the intent of scoring points with or against the advocates of public policies, positive economists are involved deeply in evaluating the consequences of policies that are either in force or are being proposed. In that public forum, and not in the strictly scientific forum, the "realism of the models" seems to be of more than immediate concern. This seems to be Samuelson's concern when, in opposition to Friedman's methodology article, he writes that it is "fundamentally wrong in thinking that unrealism in the sense of factual inaccuracy even to a tolerable degree is anything but a demerit for a theory or hypothesis (or a set of hypotheses)" (Paul Samuelson, "Problems of Methodology: Discussion," *American Economic Review*, May 1963, p. 233.

25. Friedman, "The Methodology of Positive Economics," p. 10. See also the quote in note 20.

26. Samuels, "Economics as a Science," p. 183.

27. Paul Heyne, "The Use and Abuse of the Normative-Positive Distinction" (Paper delivered at the annual meeting of the Southern Economic Association, November 1974).

28. Paul Heyne, *The Economic Way of Thinking*, 2d ed. (Chicago: Science Research Associates, 1976), p. 338.

29. Positive economists contend that since a theory is not judged by the realism of assumptions, the selection of assumptions is more or less arbitrary. They can be "unreal" and, thereby, anything. However, such a position is not fully consistent with their contention that a theory can be judged only by its *comparative* usefulness as a predictive tool. Literally, an infinite number of assumptions can be the basis of an economic theory; rationality is only one of them. If the selection of starting assumptions is completely arbitrary, unguided by the factors mentioned in this chapter, then it would appear that positive economists would continue to test in an endless manner the predictability of their theories against a wide variety of alternative theories founded on different assumptions. Some of this sort of testing is done. However, much more could be done and is not done *for good reason:* The selection of starting assumptions is not as arbitrary as they contend.

30. See Brian J. Loasby, *Choice, Complexity and Ignorance* (Cambridge: Cambridge University Press, 1976), especially chapter 11.

31. Murray N. Rothbard, *Individualism and the Philosophy of the Social Sciences* (San Francisco: Cato Institute, 1979), p. 3.

32. From personal conversations with James Buchanan, a student of Frank Knight.

33. From personal correspondence with James Buchanan.

34. Contrary to the admonitions of many strict positivists, there are conceptual limitations to any science of human action. See Frank H. Knight, "The Limitations of Scientific Method in Economics," *The Ethics of Competition* (Chicago: University of Chicago Press, 1976 [original 1935]), pp. 105–47, included in the appendix.

35. Boulding, "Economics as a Moral Science," p. 118.

36. John Rawls, *A Theory of Justice* (Cambridge, Mass.: Harvard University Press, 1971); Friedrich A. Hayek, *Law, Legislation, and Liberty,* vols. I–III (Chicago: University of Chicago Press, 1973, 1976, and 1979); James M. Buchanan, *The Limits of Liberty: Between Anarchy and Leviathan* (Chicago: University of Chicago Press, 1975); and Robert Nozick, *Anarchy, State, and Utopia* (New York: Basic Books, 1974).

6 THE ECONOMIC AND SOCIAL PHILOSOPHY OF ALBERT EINSTEIN:
A Study in Comparative Methods

Albert Einstein was both an extraordinary scientist and world personality. In a series of papers written between 1905 and 1917, he almost single-handedly dismantled and then reconstructed man's conception of the universe and, thereby, man's perception of himself. Geneticist J.B.S. Haldane once referred to Einstein as "the greatest Jew since Jesus."[1] Such a characterization is no doubt a modest overstatement; but biographer Banesh Hoffman, who wrote of Einstein's life in the context of his scientific work, reminds us that in Einstein's own time "he became a living legend, a veritable folk hero, looked upon as an oracle, entertained by royalty, statesmen, and other celebrities, and treated by public and presidents as if he were a movie star rather than a scientist."[2]

Because of his prominence as a scientist — indeed, because of the almost mystical reverence the general public held for theories it could not understand — Einstein was asked to comment on virtually every social issue of his day: racism, anti-Semitism, the nature of God, education, labor markets and unions, industrial technology, international trade and the gold standard, atomic weaponry, pacifism, world government, and even the causes of the Great Depression. All in all, he was given ample opportunity to present his views on the market economy and to offer remedies to observed social ills.

A central purpose of this chapter is to present a coherent description of Einstein's economics and social philosophy. However, there is a more fundamental reason for the study: It is to draw a connection between the modus operandi of Einstein the physicist and the social philosophy he expounded as a public figure. Although generalities are difficult to draw from a survey of the thoughts of one physicist — even a very prominent physicist — our comparison must inevitably make us wonder if the methods of physics and (free market) economics are, or can be, as similar as some economists have supposed. Perhaps the similarities exist only for physics and, say, Marxian economics, rooted in a brand of historical determinism in which subjective evaluation plays, at best, a subsidiary role, or, say, strict positive economics that posits that wants are given. We start with an exposition of Einstein's views on labor markets, technology, causes of the Great Depression, remedies for recessions, and international trade.[3]

Views on Labor Markets

Although he was vehemently opposed to the totalitarianism of Soviet communism, Einstein's theory of the labor market contains many Marxian elements. Indeed, some might suggest, with good justification, that Einstein adopted, with only minor modification, Marx's theory of labor exploitation. In his writings, Einstein suggested that exploitation of labor occurs because capitalists are able to skim off what amounts to the "surplus value of labor." Although Einstein, to my knowledge, never used the term "surplus value" specifically, he did write:

> By using the means of production, the worker produces new goods which become the property of the capitalist. The essential point about this process is the relation between what the worker produces and what he is paid, both measured in real value. Insofar as the labor contract is "free," what the worker receives is determined not by the real value of the goods he produces, but by his minimum needs and by the capitalists' requirements for labor power in relation to the number of workers competing for jobs. It is important to understand that even in theory the payment of the worker is not determined by the value of his product.[4]

These are not capricious thoughts. In his writings Einstein repeated the basic points: that labor was suppressed by competition in a capitalist society, that the labor contract was "free" (meaning, presumably, that the labor was fixed, or virtually fixed, that wages did nothing to efficiently allocate workers in the economy, and that, therefore, wages were the equivalent of rents established at minimal levels, much as Malthus hypothesized in the early part of the nineteenth century). As did Malthus and Marx, Einstein recognized that wages, for periods of time and due to fortuitous circumstances, may rise above basic needs of workers: "Labor is expensive [in the United States], because the country is sparsely inhabited in comparison with its natural resources."[5] The same is not the case in overpopulated areas such as China.[6] However, Einstein suggests, following Malthus, that high wages will result in population growth, which leads in turn to the depression of wage through competition. Furthermore, as he restated on several occasions, "everything is designed [in a capitalistic system] to save labor" when the price of labor is high.[7] The consequence is not, in Einstein's view, greater productivity and higher wages for workers, but rather the emergence of an "army of unemployed" that, through competition, leads to the suppression of labor through an emerging gap in the value of the goods produced by labor and the wages paid to labor. From these and similar comments, we have reason to conclude that Einstein's theory of the labor market was founded on a rudimentary labor theory of value (although the source of value is unclear) and subsistent wage theory, much like that developed by the early classical economists and employed by Marx in his theories of labor exploitation. The whole labor market process to Malthus, Marx, and Einstein was tied inexorably to the march of history and technological advancement.

Views on Technology

As might be expected, Einstein believed that technological advancements are spawned ultimately by basic scientific research that was not necessarily guided by the benefits of practical inventions. Technological advancements are spurred, as suggested above, by the profit incentive to minimize the use of labor. However, in Einstein's social world, technology has, to a considerable extent, a life of its own that rolls over the economic landscape, growing in the process and looming forever larger in its impact on economic and political events, as well as on the personal lives and perspectives of individuals toward the society in which they live. The technological advancements, and the productivity increases spawned by them, are to a significant extent a consequence of the capitalists' attempts to invest the "surplus" garnered from labor and, thereby, to keep the system producing at full capacity.

Einstein, like Marx, recognized that technological advances had brought about tremendous improvements in goods and services and the reduction in the difficulty of work; but, in his analysis of the market economy and world political environment, Einstein always emphasized the disruptive effects of technological advancements and the threat they posed to the future, even to the survival of mankind. He was distressed with the development of atomic technology, for which he may have felt he had been an inadvertent accomplice:

> By painful experience we have learnt that rational thinking does not suffice to solve the problems of our social life. Penetrating research and keen scientific work have often had tragic implications for mankind, producing, on the one hand, inventions which liberated man from exhausting physical labor, making life easier and richer; but on the other hand, introducing a grave restlessness into his life, making him a slave to his technological environment, and — most catastrophic of all — creating the means of his own mass destruction.[8]

In his explanation of the cause of the Great Depression, Einstein joins his rudimentary theory of labor exploitation with the ongoing advance of technology:

> As I see it, this crisis differs in character from past crises in that it is based on an entirely new set of conditions, due to the rapid progress in methods of production. Only a fraction of the available human labor in the world is needed for the production of the total amount of consumption-goods necessary to life. Under a completely free economic system this fact is bound to lead to unemployment. For reasons [basically, Malthusian reasons] which I do not propose to analyse here, the majority of people are compelled to work for the minimum wage on which life can be supported. If two factories produce the same sort of goods, other things being equal, the one will be able to produce them more cheaply which employs less workmen — i.e., makes the individual worker work as long and as hard as human nature permits. From this it follows inevitably that, with methods of production what they are today, only a fraction of the available labor can be used.[9]

Einstein reasoned that the remainder of the labor force is excluded from employment by virtue of technological advancements. Given this emerging army of unemployed and that workers' wages fall "considerably" short of the value of goods and services produced, demand does not keep pace with production: "This leads to a fall in sales and profits. Businesses go smash, which further increases unemployment and diminishes confidence in industrial concerns and therewith public participation in these mediating banks; finally the banks become insolvent through the sudden withdrawal of deposits and the wheels of industry therewith come to a complete standstill."[10] Thus, Einstein links up his theory of excessive technological development with the then newly emerging macroeconomics of John Maynard Keynes, who, we might note, developed and refined Marx's analysis of the causes of depressions.[11] As does Marx, Einstein completes his analysis of business cycles by arguing that, with the continuing advance of technology, the economy will continue to go through booms and troughs, with each succeeding trough becoming progressively worse. Political leaders will then recognize that the old economic order of capitalism is no longer compatible with the state of technology and install a new planned economy, which will, among other things, ensure an appropriate balance between aggregate supply and demand through production schedules and adjustments in the distribution of income. He wrote frequently of the up-and-down movements of the business cycle and stressed that capitalism will be undermined by unemployment that will become "increasingly chronic."[12]

As opposed to seeing the market economy as "spontaneous order" or "ordered anarchy," Einstein saw what may be termed "spontaneous disorder" or what he called "the economic anarchy of capitalistic society."[13] He saw "antagonism" where other market economists see mutual adjustments, trades, and coordination. Einstein saw in competition a process in which people, pursuing their own narrow, egoistic interests, are pitted against one another in a pervasive struggle over resources and jobs, all of which is to the detriment of all people and forces all people to disregard the common interests they share. This is partially because Einstein was an elitist to the extent that he praised efforts directed at the attainment of the common good and denigrated efforts directed exclusively at the private good: "The production and distribution of commodities is entirely unorganized [under capitalism] so that everybody must live in fear of being eliminated from the economic cycle, in this way suffering for the want of everything . . . This is due to the fact that the intelligence and the character of the masses are incomparably lower than the intelligence and character of the few who [like Mozart, his favorite musician] produce something valuable for the community."[14]

The ongoing dialectical rub between technology and social institutions would not, necessarily, in Einstein's social model be resolved by revolution. Although he felt people had a moral duty to fight Hitlerism, Einstein was fundamentally a pacifist and looked to peaceful means of changing social institutions. In this regard, he felt people of prominence have a moral obligation to work for peaceful reform by speaking out on the issues, showing people the absurdity of any economic system that bases production on "profit, not use." He also wanted to change the educational system to emphasize social, as opposed to individual, values and to promote collective, rather than individual, solutions to production problems. In short, he sought approaches that deal with production and distribution problems in a more "humane," "rational," and "less anarchistic" manner. His support of socialism was in part founded upon the view that

> unlimited competition leads to a huge waste of labor, and to that crippling of the social consciousness of individuals which I mentioned before . . . This crippling of individuals I consider the worst evil of capitalism. Our whole educational system suffers from this evil. An exaggerated competitive attitude is inculcated into the student, who is trained to worship acquisitive success as a preparation for this future career.[15]

Einstein also believed that modern technology was responsible for the moral debasement of the individual and dehumanization of the individual through repetitive work. He once wrote to his friend Otto Juliusburger, a psychiatrist trapped in Hitler's Berlin,

> I think we have to safeguard ourselves against people who are a menace to others, quite apart from what may have motivated their deeds. What need is there for a criterion of responsibility? I believe that the horrifying deterioration in the ethical conduct of people today stems primarily from the mechanization and dehumanization of our lives — a disastrous byproduct of the development of the scientific and technical mentality. Nostra culpa. I don't see any way to tackle this disastrous short-coming. Man grows old faster than the planet he inhabits.[16]

Finally, Einstein saw growth in technology as the cause of the concentration in modern industry. This theme was especially crystallized on two occasions, first when he was responding to Soviet scientists' criticism of his proposed world government and later when he was attempting to make the case for socialism:

[1] If the socio-economic problem is considered objectively, it appears as follows: technological development has led to increasing centralization of the economic mechanism. It is this development which is also responsible for the fact that economic power in all widely industrialized countries has become concentrated in the hands of the relatively few. These people, in capitalist countries, do not need to account for their actions to the public as a whole; they must do so in socialist countries in which they are civil servants to those who exercise political power.[17]

[2] Private capital tends to become concentrated in a few hands, partly because of competition among the capitalists and partly because technological developments and the increasing division of labor encourage the formation of larger units of production at the expense of the smaller ones. The result of these developments is an oligarchy of private capital the enormous power of which cannot be effectively checked even by democratically organized political society.[18]

Regardless of what underlay his thinking, Einstein was very concerned that the concentration of economic power in the hands of a few would lead to political control by the few. He was also concerned that the concentration of economic power meant control of the educational process:

The centralization of production has brought about a concentration of productive capital in the hands of a relatively small number of citizens of the land. This small group exerts overwhelming domination over institutions for the education of our youth as well as the great newspapers of the country . . . The dominant economic minority, heretofore autonomous and responsible to no one, has placed itself in opposition to this limitation of its freedom of action, demanded for the good of the whole people. For its defense this minority is resorting to every known legal method at its disposal. We need not, therefore, be surprised that they are using their preponderant influence on the schools and the press to prevent youth from being enlightened on this problem which is so vital to the sound and peaceful development of life in this country.[19]

Einstein's apparent hostility to capitalists may be understood, if not fully appreciated, if it is remembered that, fearing a price had been placed on his head, he had to flee Germany and a regime that was associated with the probusiness political right.

Remedies for Recession

To remedy the economic malaise of his times (mainly, the economic difficulties encountered during the 1930s), Einstein proposed the development of a planned economy and offered, in different places and on different occasions, five policy options:

(1) Reduce the workweek of all employees so that unemployment will be "systematically abolished."[20] The problem with this policy proposal is self-evident to a market economist. However, if Einstein were ever told of these objections, he would probably have remained unperturbed. First, he had little confidence in economics because so much of "human history has — as is well known - been largely influenced by causes which are by no means exclusively economic in nature."[21]

Second, he very likely would have argued that fully employed people do not really need all that they can buy with their incomes. And, third, any harm done to some would be counterbalanced by the benefits received by those who would then be employed, if only for a part of the workweek. He reasoned that, in order to be happy, people must have an opportunity to think and to develop themselves in nonmaterial ways; to do that, only their basic needs must be met. In an essay "On Freedom," he wrote that two goals can be agreed upon:

1. Those instrumental goods which should serve to maintain the life and health of all human beings should be produced by the least possible labor of all. 2. The satisfaction of physical needs is, indeed, the indispensable precondition of a satisfactory existence, but in itself it is not enough. In order to be content men must also have the possibility of developing their intellectual and artistic powers to whatever extent is in accord with their personal characteristics and abilities.[22]

And he added that "man should not have to work for the achievement of the necessities of life to such an extent that he has neither time nor strength for personal activities. Without this second kind of outward liberty, freedom of expression is useless for him . . . The development of science and of the creative activities of the spirit in general requires still another kind of freedom . . . It is the freedom of the spirit which consists in the independence of thought from the restrictions of authoritarian and social prejudices as well as from unphilosophical routinizing and habit in general."[23] In short, Einstein saw a form of liberation of the human spirit in restrictions on the market.

(2) Set minimum wages "in such a way that the purchasing power of the workers keeps pace with production."[24] As pointed out in an earlier section, workers in capitalistic systems are paid less than the value of their production. Capitalists who, in Einstein's view, could not possibly use all their income for consumption must invest to keep aggregate demand in line with production and to keep the economy going. However, the growth in worker productivity might, from time to time, surge ahead to the point that total demand would fall short of total production. As we have seen, this is what Einstein thought was the case in Germany, as well as the United States, in the 1930s:

I do not believe that the remedy for our present difficulties lies in a knowledge of productive capacity and consumption, because this knowledge is likely, in the main, to come too late. Moreover, the trouble in Germany seems to me to be not hypertrophy of the machinery of production but deficient purchasing power in a large section of the population, which has been cast out of the productive process through rationalization.[25]

According to Einstein's theory, his proposed rise in minimum wages would spread out purchasing power among people and increase consumption, thus stimulating economic activity — a familiar Keynesian proposition.

(3) "Further," writes Einstein, "in those industries which have become monopolistic in character through organization on the part of the producers, prices must be controlled by the state in order to keep the creation of new capital within reasonable bounds and prevent the artificial strangling of production and consumption."[26] Einstein was concerned that monopoly profits lead to investment (since the owners do not know what else to do with their money) and thereby to advancements in technology and productivity. As we have seen, technological improvements in Einstein's model of the economy lead to a gap between production and purchasing power, reduced employment, and a downward self-accelerating movement in the level of economic activity. By controlling monopoly prices, Einstein contended, the state could effectively temper technological advancements and would retard, if not eliminate, the periodic emergence of deflationary gaps between output and aggregate demand.

(4) Exclude older people from "certain sorts of work (which I call 'unqualified' work), receiving instead a certain income, as having by that time done enough work of a kind accepted by society as productive."[27] The purpose of this proposal was to ensure young people a part in the productive process, giving them not only income but responsibility, a sense of self-worth, and a role in meeting the needs of the community.

(5) Control the money supply and the volume of credit "in such a way as to keep the price-level steady, all protection being abolished."[28] Since this recommendation was made during the Great Depression, we might surmise that Einstein was concerned about deflation, not inflation. At one time he did recommend that we go off the gold standard because decreases in gold reserves lead to contractions in the money supply that have adverse economic consequences. He felt, because of the inflexibility of gold stocks, international reserves should be tied to something other than gold:

> I am also of the opinion that fluctuations in the value of the money must be avoided by substituting for the gold standard a standard based on certain classes of goods selected according to the conditions of consumption — as Keynes, if I am not mistaken, long ago proposed. With the introduction of this system one might consent to a certain amount of "inflation," as compared with the present monetary situation, if one could believe that the state would really make rational use of the windfall thus accruing to it.[29]

With these types of controls, Einstein believed that "it might be possible to establish a proper balance between production and consumption without too great a limitation of free enterprise, and at the same time to stop the intolerable tyranny of the owners of the means of production (land, machinery) over the wage earners, in the widest sense of the term.''[30]

Views on World Trade

Einstein's comments on international trade were sparse. However, his views on the subject were consistent with arguments already developed on the consequences of technological advancements. He pointed out that because of its reliance on free enterprise and its inability to match domestic output with domestic demand,

> the United States is compelled to emphasize her export trade. Without it, she could not permanently keep her total productive machinery fully utilized. These conditions would not be harmful if the exports were balanced by imports of about the same value. Exploitation of foreign nations would then consist in the fact that the labor value of imports would considerably exceed that of our exports. However, every effort is being made to avoid this, since almost every import would make a part of the productive machinery idle.[31]

The Philosophical Triangle: Physics, Economics, and Dostoevsky

What are the philosophical, social, and scientific sources of Einstein's views on economics? Why did he espouse economic views that many market economists consider patently absurd? These questions emerge each time we consider a theoretical cornerstone of Einstein's social commentary. Perhaps, the latter question is unfair; it presumes that Einstein was wrong in his interpretation of social events. Still, the question is worth asking, and several tentative answers can be offered.

Personal Situation and History

A *partial* answer is not difficult to discern. Einstein was a very busy person. He spent most of his time in his middle and later years participating in the debate over Neil Bohr's statistical theory of quantum mechanics and attempting to construct, unsuccessfully, a unified field theory. He probably had little time to study economic questions in a thorough and penetrating manner. However, such an explanation largely begs the question. We are concerned here with the predisposition of the scientific mind to look at social forces, predicated in a mixed fashion upon historical determinism and upon free individual (incentive-driven) decisions, as disharmonizing and to accept readily facile conclusions. In the case of Einstein, the acceptance of a Marxian perspective of economic events can be explained in part by his personal history, by his identification with the plight of Jews in general, and, most importantly, by his philosophy of science that elevates universal harmony (and the discovery of that harmony) to an ethical standard for judging the justice of a social system. As might be expected, Einstein's physics was inextricably entangled in his social pronunciation.

Einstein's condemnation of the capitalistic system — its tendency toward monopolization, exploitation of labor, and self-destruction — may be explained in a limited way by his personal history. Einstein grew up during the last quarter of the nineteenth century, a period noted for a growth in technology (especially in chemistry and electricity) that allowed more efficient production on a larger scale. In Germany this period was also marked by the growth of new firms, by the consolidation of small firms into larger production units, and by the competitive demise of many small firms, including three businesses organized by Einstein's father. Concern over trusts in the 1880s and 1890s was as much a political issue in Germany as it was in the United States.

Further, as biographer Ronald Clark notes, Zurich, where Einstein took his first job as a patent inspector third-class, was a haven for exiled German and Russian revolutionaries like Trotsky, Rosa Luxemburg, Alexander Koolontai, and Lenin.[32] The intellectual openness of Zurich to socialism no doubt contributed to Einstein's social-political education. This education was completed by his very good friend, Friedrich Adler, who was the son of the leader of the Austrian Social Democrats and who later became a significant force in Europe's revolutionary socialist movement.

Sense of Community

As a socialist, Einstein was attracted by the thought of mankind as a "community" bound together by common predilection, values, and goals. Personally, however, he was a loner who jealously guarded his individuality. He wore his hair extraordinarily long, giving it little attention, and he often dressed sloppily and went to work without wearing socks. In his social philosophy, Einstein was for the most part unconcerned with outward appearances. Peculiarly, and somewhat contradictorily, he was an individualist as well as a socialist.[33] His social philosophy was anchored in a concern with "social justice," a concept that Einstein only vaguely defined:

> Not until the creation and maintenance of decent conditions of life for all men are recognized and accepted as a common obligation of all men and all countries — not until then shall we, with a certain degree of justification be able to speak of mankind as civilized.[34]

The common obligation of *all* people to be concerned with *all* others, which is the essence of Einstein's concept of social justice, is a central theme that comes through in his writings time and time again: "For looked at from a simple human point of view, moral conduct does not mean merely a stern demand to renounce some of the desired joys of life, but rather a sociable interest in a happier lot for all men''[35] Einstein was strongly opposed to capitalism, in part because he saw capitalism as an affront to the moral and ''sociable interest'' of each person to be concerned about the ''happier lot for all men.'' Einstein felt capitalism elevates the private interests of the individual in his own personal welfare and denigrates the collective interests of the individual in the welfare of the community. For this concept of social justice, Einstein found a cultural, quasi-religious foundation in Judaism: ''The bond that has united the Jews for thousands of years and that unites them today is, above all, the democratic ideal of mutual aid and tolerance among all men.''[36] Einstein obviously admired Jews like Moses, Spinoza, and Marx — individuals he specifically cites — because they ''all lived and sacrificed themselves for the ideal of social justice,'' which Einstein believed was a cultural response to their Jewish heritage. Einstein saw his own socialist leanings as part and parcel of the Jewish sense of community, a tradition inculcated in the Jewish consciousness by centuries of persecution.[37]

Religion

Einstein was not religious in the traditional sense. From his religious training, which was largely pro forma, he concluded quite early, at the age of 12, that most of what was written in the *Bible* was inspired by aggressive imaginations.[38] He did not believe in a God that meddled in the daily lives of people. He saw such a conception of God as being incompatible with the purpose of science, which is to search for the fundamental laws of the universe. In answer to a sixth grader's question, ''Do scientists pray?'' Einstein responded,

> Scientific research is based on the idea that *everything that takes place is determined by laws of nature, and therefore this holds for the actions of people.* For this reason, a research scientist will hardly be inclined to believe that events could be influenced by a prayer, i.e., by a wish addressed to a supernatural Being. [emphasis added][39]

He went on to explain to the little girl that the scientist's belief in all-pervasive laws, many of which can be ascertained by human beings, is necessarily founded upon a faith in some power enormously greater than the power of the scientist who seeks to understand the universe. ''In this way,'' Einstein added, ''the pursuit of science leads to religious feeling of a special sort, which is indeed quite different from the religiosity of someone more naive.''[40]

Einstein's deistic conception of God is succinctly expressed in his often quoted remark ''God does not play dice with the universe.'' This remark, as it turns out, says as much about his approach to physics as it does about his approach to religion. Einstein was absolutely convinced that all events in the universe through time could potentially be explained by scientific laws. The essential problem facing the scientist is to discover those laws and state them in a way that is comprehensible to other human beings. In short, Einstein believed in universal determinism.[41] The outward, ballooning movements of the galaxies within the universe are set for all time. Further, it follows, in Einstein's view of the social world, that the futures of individuals are as determined (by the laws that are fixed) as their pasts, meaning that there is no such thing as viable free will, a point he made with force in a letter to his friend Juliusburger in 1946: "You take a definite stand about Hitler's responsibility. I myself have never really believed in the subtler distinctions that lawyers foist upon physicians. Objectively, there is, after all, no free will."[42]

Natural Harmony

The natural harmony of the universe — which is the consequence of the workings of inextricably entangled laws — is, to Einstein, the ultimate expression of beauty, something to gaze upon in total wonder and humility as a work of art. Einstein wrote:

> It is the cosmic religious feeling that gives a man strength of this sort [to endure the many failures in the search for scientific principles]. A contemporary has said, not unjustly, that in this materialistic age of ours the serious scientific workers are the only profoundly religious people.

He added elsewhere that the scientist's

> religious feeling takes the form of rapturous amazement at the harmony of natural law, which reveals an intelligence of such superiority that, compared with it, all the systematic thinking and acting of human beings is an utterly insignificant reflection. This principle is the guiding principle of his life and work, insofar as he succeeds in keeping himself from the shackles of selfish desires.[43]

The natural harmony was, in Einstein's mind, the ultimate controlling force and the ultimate destiny of the universe. In a real sense, it was Einstein's God who gave purpose to his own scientific search and concern for a social order and harmony.[44] The natural harmony is the ultimate ethical value that transformed his mechanical scientific search of what *is* into a statement of what *should be:* Natural harmony is both that which *is* and that which *should be*.

Einstein was distressed with Bohr's statistical theory of quantum mechanics simply because it cannot explain and predict each and every event of each and every electron revolving around the nucleus of an atom. The theory can only predict the probable position of the electron at any point in time. Again, for Einstein, God does not play dice, shoot craps, or send electrons randomly around the core of an atom. Although he was unable to provide a better theory and was willing to accept Bohr's as a stopgap device that reflects the imperfect state of scientific knowledge, until he died Einstein maintained the faith that some law exists to predict the events in the atom. To Einstein, the craving for universal harmony (meaning orderliness established by laws) of the macrocosm must be predicated upon a similar harmony within the microscosm of the atom. Further, the harmony of the two cosms must be joined in a grand harmonious scheme for the entire universe. He was convinced that it is "logically possible to establish such rigorous laws that they demand uniquely determined constants, whose numerical values could not be changed without destroying the theory."[45]

The euclidian conception of the universe, which preceded Einstein's theory of relativity, permitted a harmonious vision of the macrocosm without a necessary harmony of events within the independent components of the microcosm. The new, noneuclidian conception of the universe establishes an interdependence among all components within the universe — time, space, mass, and energy — because, after all, the components are relative; the laws of the universe must be the same from the perspective of the atom as well as from the perspective of a person approaching the speed of light. Some have concluded from reading Einstein that everything in his theories is relative — nothing is absolute. This is not the case. *Complete* harmony, to Einstein, is the one invariant standard — *the* ethical standard — on which all other conceptions of order must be founded and from which all events must be judged.

Dostoevsky

Einstein once commented that Russian novelist Fyodor Dostoevsky — author of *Crime and Punishment, The Possessed, The Idiot, The Raw Youth, The Brothers Karamazov,* and other works — "gave me more than any thinker, more than Guass."[46] In that statement is the necessary clue for linking Einstein's science with his social philosophy. Dostoevsky's novels generally deal with human suffering, but, as Boris Kuznetsov stresses, they are concerned with one over-riding question: "Can there be universal harmony if the fate of any individual is ignored, if any individual is a victim of the social system?"[47] Of course, the novelist's answer is that there cannot be. The system is not moral — in the sense of being harmonious — unless the fate of *every* individual is considered. Einstein agreed, and his agreement reflects the extension of his physics into discussions of the morality of the capitalistically dominated social system. To Einstein, the actions and fate of each individual must be synchronized with the actions and fate of all others in order for complete social harmony to exist — and in order for complete universal harmony to exist. The fates of individuals — and the events they represent — cannot be left to chance any more than the fates of electrons within an atom can be left to chance and still have universal harmony. The attraction of Dostoevsky to Einstein was, as summarized by Kuznetsov, that the

> essence of his [Dostoevsky's] art is an appeal addressed to the twentieth century; man needs a social and moral harmony that does not ignore local disharmonies and refuses to accept the individual sufferings of any man, a harmony that leaves no place for coercion, oppression, or contempt for the weak.[48]

Further, Einstein's social philosophy was founded upon the view that each person has two dimensions: One is the egoistic dimension that seeks pleasure and avoids pain, and the other is the social dimension that strives to become involved in the lives and fates of other individuals.[49] He believed that under capitalism, however, competition destroys people's social concerns: "Everything is dominated by the cult of efficiency and of success and not by the value of things and men in relation to the moral ends of human society. To that must be added the moral deterioration resulting from the ruthless economic struggle."[50] A worker cannot be concerned about the welfare of others simply because he is, as pointed out earlier, forced to accept a subsistence wage. If a worker helps someone else or is concerned with the establishment of the "goals of society," he runs the risk of falling below a subsistence livelihood. The individual entrepreneur must realize that being concerned about the welfare of others and taking such concern into account in production decisions will incur higher production costs and will therefore incur the risk of being eliminated from the market by lower-cost competitors. As Einstein might have said, we are all the products of a social process and we are, as a consequence, social beings; and universal harmony depends upon people playing their roles as social animals and being concerned about the welfare of *every* other person. Capitalism, as an institutional form, is immoral in Einstein's world simply because it denies people the opportunity to be concerned about others; it therefore promotes *disharmony* and is an affront to Einstein's invariant ethical standard.

Individual Freedom

As odd as it may seem, Einstein revered individual freedom. He once wrote that a discovery — scientific, artistic, or otherwise — can be made only by a free person; and on another occasion he added:

> If we want to resist the powers which threaten to suppress intellectual and individual freedom, we must keep clearly before us what is at stake, and what we owe to that freedom which our ancestors have won for us after hard struggles. Without such freedom

there would have been no Shakespeare, no Goethe, no Newton, no Faraday, no Pasteur, and no Lister. There would be no comfortable houses for the masses of the people, no railway, no wireless, no protection against epidemics, no cheap books, no culture and no enjoyment of art for all.[51]

Einstein's concept of freedom does not conflict completely with his views on universal determinism and the capitalistic system. True freedom to Einstein is not the outward manifestation of what people can do with things or with themselves, which is the type of freedom conceptualized for the workings of free markets. Rather, true freedom is essentially intellectual; it involves the release of the individual from worldly or materialistic concerns to the contemplation of ideas — the magic of the "mysterious" order of the universe — or the development of artistic qualities and abilities. Freedom is the ability to create knowledge of oneself and one's surroundings.[52]

To Einstein, the appropriate model of man is *homo cogitan*, the reflective and resourceful thinker, not *homo economicus*, the maximizing producer and trader.[53] A certain amount of material comforts are necessary in order for man to aspire to the status of *homo cogitan*, the truly free person, but that does not mean the entire economic system must be organized to ensure efficient production. Indeed, as has been pointed out, an economic system organized to produce efficiently will, in Einstein's view of the world, enslave individuals to the mundane concerns of getting more and more for themselves — a system that can never be completely satisfying, or as satisfying as the quest for knowledge. As stated earlier, Einstein does not view controls on the market economy and collective attempts to distribute income more evenly as denials of freedom; on the contrary, they are the road to freedom — inner freedom, that is — and to the liberation of the social tendency of man, which is inspired by the development of knowledge.

In summary, market economists may disagree with Einstein's assessment of the capitalistic system simply because they — economists and Einstein — do not start with the same a priori conception of the essential nature of freedom. Furthermore, because of their differences over the concept of freedom, they necessarily differ over the meaning of efficiency. Efficiency to economists is the welfare improvement experienced by traders because of the trades they "freely" choose to make. Efficiency to Einstein is the welfare improvement people experience when they are liberated from the necessity of "making ends meet" and are able to engage in reflective thought, which ultimately produces concern about the welfare of others.

Einstein's views on freedom and universal determinism cannot be fully reconciled. He makes little or no effort to tell us how people, whose every action is predetermined by universal laws, can ever be free in any meaningful sense of the term. He does not tell us why we should even care about the fate of mankind if our futures are as determined as our pasts. Perhaps, if asked to address these problems,

Einstein would respond by saying that our actions may be determined but our thoughts are not and that we can experience freedom intellectually if not physically. However, such a position begs the question of why we should be concerned about the workings of the capitalistic system if nothing can be changed and people do not have at least a modicum of control over their own destinies.

Concluding Comments

Einstein's criticisms of the capitalistic economy — which, as we have seen, tend to be Marxian — were legion. Contrary to the admonitions of Marx, however, Einstein never advocated revolution. Instead, he advocated a change in the educational system to instill social and community values, a change that would eventually lead to the political demise of capitalism, to the rise of a planned world economy, and to the enlargement of individual freedom as he defined it. How would the political and educational systems be wrested from the control of the capitalists? How would a planned economy operate — on a daily or yearly basis? How would government, empowered to plan the entire economy, be controlled? These are critical questions that Einstein asked but made little attempt to answer.

Notes

1. Nigel Calder, *Einstein's Universe* (New York: Viking Press, 1979), p. 1.
2. Banesh Hoffman, *Albert Einstein: Creator or Rebel* (New York: Viking Press, 1973), p. 3.
3. Critical examination of a physicist's economics can be readily criticized by way of a question, "Who cares about Einstein's economics? Is anyone especially concerned with Paul Samuelson's physics?" There are three possible answers. First, the study of Einstein's economics can be conducted as a matter of interest, just to see what an important scientist thought on matters not directly related to his profession. Second, as noted in the text, we may be able to learn something about the way the man thought about all issues. And third, while it is true that not many people are especially concerned about Paul Samuelson's physics, it is also true that he has not devoted very much of his professional life to writing on the subject. Perhaps, if he had spent more time writing on topics in physics, how and why he thought about physics *and* economics would be of interest to both economists and physicists.
4. Albert Einstein, *Out of My Later Years* (Secaucus, N.J.: Citadel Press, 1976), p. 128–29.
5. Albert Einstein, *The World as I See It* (Secaucus, N.J.: Citadel Press, n.d.), p. 38.
6. Einstein, *Out of My Later Years,* p. 129.
7. Einstein, *The World as I See It,* p. 38.
8. Ibid., p. 152.
9. Ibid., p. 70.
10. Ibid., pp. 70–71.
11. Ibid., p. 77.
12. In his defense of socialism, Einstein once wrote:

I am convinced that there is only *one* way to eliminate these grave evils [of capitalism], namely through the establishment of a socialist economy, accompanied by the educational system which would be oriented toward social goals. In such an economy, the means of production are owned by society itself and are utilized in a planned fashion. A planned economy, which adjusts production to the needs of the community, would distribute the work to be done among all those able to work and would guarantee a livelihood to every man, woman, and child. The education of the individual, in addition to promoting his own innate abilities, would attempt to develop in him a sense of responsibility for his fellow men in place of the glorification of the power and success in our present society. [*Out of My Later Years*, p. 130]

13. Einstein, *Out of My Later Years*, p. 128.

14. Einstein's disdain for creature comforts is apparent throughout his writings:

Comfort and happiness have never appeared to me as a goal. I call these ethical bases the ideals of the swineherd . . . The commonplace goals of human endeavor — possessions, outward success and luxury — have always seemed to me despicable, since early youth. [as requoted in A.P. French, ed., *Einstein: A Centenary Volume* (Cambridge, Mass.: Harvard University Press, 1979), p. 217]

On another occasion Einstein repeated his central theme that capitalism lacks central direction and, therefore, must be unorganized, anarchistic:

Mechanical means of production in an unorganized economy have had the result that a substantial proportion of mankind is no longer needed for the production of goods and is thus excluded from the process of economic circulation. The immediate consequences are the weakening of purchasing power and the devaluation of labor because of excessive competition, and these give rise, at ever shortening intervals, to grave paralysis in the production of goods. Ownership of the means of production, on the other hand, carries a power to which the traditional safeguards of our political institutions are unequal. Mankind is caught up in a struggle for adoption to these new conditions — a struggle that may bring true liberation, if our generation shows itself equal to the task. [*Out of My Later Years*, p. 136]

15. Ibid.

16. Albert Einstein, *Albert Einstein: The Human Side*, Helen Dukes and Banesh Hoffman, eds. (Princeton, N.J.: Princeton University Press, 1979), p. 82.

17. Einstein, *Out of My Later Years*, p. 170.

18. Ibid., p. 129.

19. Einstein, *The World as I See It*, p. 73.

20. Einstein, *Out of My Later Years*, p. 123.

21. Ibid.

22. Ibid., p. 12.

23. Ibid., p. 13.

24. Einstein, *The World as I See It*, p. 73.

25. Ibid. , p. 75.

26. Ibid., p. 74.

27. Ibid., p. 77.

28. Ibid., p. 76.

29. Ibid., p. 77.

30. Ibid., p. 74.

31. Einstein, *Out of My Later Years*, pp. 173–74.

32. Ronald W. Clark, *Einstein: The Life and Times* (New York: Avon Books, 1971), chapters 1–3.

33. Einstein once wrote:

There is one other thing which follows from that conception — that we must not only tolerate differences between individuals and between groups, but we should indeed welcome them and look upon them as enriching our existence. That is the essence of true tolerance; without tolerance in this widest sense there can be no question of true morality. [Ibid., p. 19]

34.   Ibid., pp. 258–59.
35.   Ibid., p. 19.
36.   Ibid., p. 249.
37.   Ibid.
38.   Albert Einstein, "Autobiographical Notes," *Albert Einstein: Philosopher-Scientist,* Paul Arthur Schlipp, ed. (Evanston, Ill.: Library of Living Philosophers, 1949), p. 5.
39.   Ibid., p. 32.
40.   Ibid., p. 33.
41.   Einstein wrote, "But the scientist is possessed by the sense of universal causation. The future, to him, is very white as necessary and determined as the past." (*The World As I See It,* p. 29)
42.   Einstein, *The Human Side,* p. 81.
43.   Einstein, *The World as I See It,* p. 29.
44.   Einstein said as much: "This deep intuitive conviction of the existence of a higher power of thought which manifests itself in the inscrutable universe represents the content of my definition of God" (As quoted in Clark, *Einstein,* p. 168). In 1955 Abba Eban, the Israel ambassador to the United Nations, drew a strong connection between Judaism and the quest for universal harmony when he wrote:

The Hebrew mind has been obsessed for centuries by a concept of order and harmony in the universal design. The search for laws hitherto unknown which govern cosmic forces; the doctrine of a relative harmony in nature; the idea of a calculable relationship between matter and energy — these are all more likely to emerge from a basic Hebrew philosophy and turn of mind that from many others.

Ronald Clark, from whose work the quotation is taken, adds:

This may sound like hindsight plus special pleading; yet the long line of Jewish physicians from the nineteenth century, and the even longer list of those who later sought the underlying unifications of the subatomic world, give it a plausibility which cannot easily be contested. [Clark, *Einstein: The Life and Times* p. 36]

45.   Einstein, "Autobiographical Notes," p. 63. For extended discussions of the role of harmony in Einstein's connection of the universe, see Gerald Holton, "What Precisely Is 'Thinking'? Einstein's Answer," *Albert Einstein: A Centenary Volume,* pp. 153–67; Boris Kuznetsov, "Einstein, Science and Culture," *Albert Einstein: A Centenary Volume,* pp. 167–84; Francois Russo, "The Philosopher-Scientist, Einstein," in Louis de Broglie, Louis Armand, and Pierre Henri-Simon, eds. (New York: Peebles Press, 1979), pp. 173–94; and Virgil G. Hinshaw, "Einstein's Social Philosopher," *Albert Einstein: Philosopher-Scientist,* pp. 649–61.
46.   Kuznetsov, "Einstein , Science and Culture," p. 178.
47.   Ibid.
48.   Boris Kuznetsov, *Einstein and Dostoevsky* (London: Hutchinson Educational, 1972), pp. 15–20.
49.   Einstein, *Out of My Later Years,* pp. 15–20.
50.   Ibid., p. 18.
51.   Ibid., p. 149.
52.   Einstein, "Autobiographical Notes," p. 5.
53.   Commenting on Einstein's social philosophy, Boris Kuznetsov has written:

Knowledge is a liberation, a growth and realization of internal freedom; this is the definition of man, *homo cogitans,* the process of cultural development. Or more exactly, it is the substratum that makes this cultural development irreversible. ["Einstein, Science and Culture," p. 178]

POSTSCRIPT

Methodological discussions, while valuable, have one unfortunate feature: They can be interminable. Knowing where to conclude even a small volume like this one is not always easy. Critics abound, and to try to make the argument "airtight" is tempting and, of course, impossible. Foregoing chapters have stirred a modest degree of controversy, and to the critics I am indebted.[1] They have helped clarify issues that may have otherwise remained unsettled in my own way of thinking.

Their writings have also shown how easy it is in the area of methodology to talk at cross-purposes. Let me attempt to summarize a number of the foregoing arguments using, admittedly, a radically different approach. Perhaps, variation in the presentation will add clarity to my own position and make a brief extension of the discussion useful. In this concluding chapter, I quote extensively from published comments because my purpose is to provide, to the extent possible, the full flavor of the criticisms.

Conceptual vs. Practical Limits to Science

To the suggestion that all behavior may not have a "rational" basis, Professor Michael Watts has articulated a familiar theme:

> There is no quarrel here that wants and tastes are sometimes, perhaps often, formed in the

This is a revised version of an article that appeared in the April 1981 issue of *Southern Economic Journal*. Reprinted with permission of the publisher.

non-rational domain. But values are not wants and tastes, and though values admittedly do influence the formation of wants and tastes they do not have to be formed or "discovered" in the same way, or in the same domain of rationality or non-rationality. Also, there is no reason why individuals who establish their values rationally may not, at least on many occasions, irrationally establish tastes and preferences — the sincere Christian may buy pet rocks, worthless swamplands in Florida, or even pornographic magazines.

Values may be, on occasion, formed irrationally, just as consumers may, on occasion, make an irrational choice even when the relevant incomes, prices and tastes are evident and well understood. Inexperienced and mentally handicapped individuals are more likely to establish values irrationally, just as they are more likely to make irrational purchases in the marketplace. As the great majority of individuals mature, however, they do come to "know themselves," and to revise those values which are not consistent with some admittedly internally developed picture of themselves. Perhaps we are not all quite so rational as Socrates in establishing our values, but it is more likely that we are simply not as bright in tracing out the long-term consequences of the values we have rationally chosen to adopt at some point in our lives.

It may be, as McKenzie claims, that we choose values like the person who is set down in the middle of a densely forested mountain range and is told to climb the highest peak. The process of forming values is perhaps inevitably difficult, frustrating, and at times confusing. But, if we were to set Stigler, Becker, McKenzie or most any group of mature individuals down in that forest it seems a safe bet that they would adopt some rational method to find even the most elusive summit. A decision is made no less rationally because it is difficult — quite possibly decisions are made more carefully and rationally when they are difficult.

McKenzie suggests that "economic inquiry may be able to partially penetrate the realm of human experience in which values are formed." And Knight has said most boldly that "the general theory of economics is . . . simply the rationale of life. — In so far as it has any rationale." McKenzie has eloquently pointed out some of the limits of economic analysis, but to the extent that the process of forming values is a rational one he is also making a compelling case to extend the boundaries of that analysis into truly unconventional areas. Extending boundaries must always be done cautiously, especially where questions of value are involved; but, methodologically, if economists' only prerequisite for formal inquiry is rational behavior, there are new and different mountains to be climbed as soon as a few new pieces of equipment are developed, or purchased from those who have already explored the territory.[2]

Professor Tibor Machan is concerned that I may have misrepresented Gary Becker's view of economics as a science. Machan writes:

> Strictly put, the point attributed to Becker, based on the quoted remarks, is not as ambitious as McKenzie thinks. It means, simply, that all human behavior has aspects conducive to economic inquiry, or, all human behavior has economic aspects. And this claim can be true while it could also be true that all human behavior has noneconomic aspects as well. Furthermore, it could be true that for some purposes focusing on noneconomic aspects will be more important than focusing on economic ones.[3]

Machan later adds clarifying points:

> Several reasons can be adduced toward the rejections of McKenzie's conclusion, despite what appears on its face to be irrefutable evidence. First, Becker's claims do not mean the strong position McKenzie ascribes to them. While all of what Becker believes can yield to the economic approach may indeed so yield, some of the topics could well yield more readily to a different, perhaps yet unidentified or not very widely embraced, but better approach. In addition, Becker has said that there is a possibility that some other approach could lead to a better understanding of some human behavior than can be obtained via the economic approach. In effect, then, Becker's thesis is that all human behavior may be approached by way of economic analysis and as far as it is known today this is the most promising approach to all human behavior. Yet it is possible that this will not remain the case. Should there be some approach to the systematic study of some human behavior that is more fruitful than those Becker is aware of — a possibility warranted on the basis of reading his work, he would be wrong about what is the best approach.[4]

Although the names Gary Becker and George Stigler arose from time to time in my essays, especially chapter 3, their particular economics is not the crux of my argument. Their works are merely used as a convenient means of raising what I consider to be an overriding methodological question confronting the "imperialistic economics" of the 1970s; namely, Are there *conceptual,* as opposed to *practical,* limits to economics as a scientific discipline? Many economists, following in the intellectual footsteps of Becker and Stigler, seem to think that the scientific boundaries of economics can only be established by the purely practical application of the "tools of analyses" to an ever-widening arena of human activity. The implicit and, at times, explicit assumption has been that from a strictly conceptual perspective, there are no limits. Implicit in this position — which is fully reflected in Stigler and Becker's "De Gustabus Non Est Disputandum" — is the belief that methodologies of science can and must be judged ultimately by those very same methodologies that are the object of dispute. Throughout the book I have attempted, albeit somewhat indirectly, to question the appropriateness of such an approach to judging the extended applicability of science.

Furthermore, I have tried to argue that there are necessarily *conceptual* barriers to any science founded upon the concept of "rationality." (I am here willing to accept Professor Machan's suggestion that rationality is an a priori statement about what people *will* do, and not just what they are able to do, an adjustment to my position that, in my view, makes my argument stronger.)[5] Actually, I am fully sympathetic with the view that people operate within several levels of rationality, but the central point is that neoclassical positivism requires a very special and quite specific form of rational behavior, one in which the goods and the bads are well defined and well known by the individual and the researcher. Empirical verification, if nothing else, necessitates this. Such conceptual limitations do not deny us the right to extend the domain of science, but they do suggest that we should be cautious in interpreting the importance of what we learn from the extended application of science. In this regard I cannot agree more with Professor Watts. Conceptual limitations require that we judge the applicability of science by more than the ability of the "model to make correct predictions," the essence of much of what has been said.

As opposed to recounting points readily available in the foregoing chapters, let me redevelop my argument regarding the conceptual limitations of science with a relevant, though somewhat extreme, extension of economics to an important area of human behavior. One can imagine the tools of economic analysis being applied to human sexual behavior. Economists might model such behavior either by mathematics, incorporating sets of simultaneous interactive equations manipulated by way of bordered Hessians and the like, or with elaborate graphical techniques, involving production functions, indifference curves, and so forth. The hypotheses deduced can, conceivably, be tested with available data on people's demand and cost functions and coital frequency. However, after all is said and done, regardless of the "predictability" of the model, cannot one rightly question the usefulness and importance of the analysis — just how much of human behavior is "explained" or "understood" through the applications of scientific techniques? While such scientific analysis may be interesting and perhaps amusing, should we really expect science to make, regardless of how much time and attention were applied to the problem by scientists, much of a contribution to ur commonsense understandings of what people do? If strict positivists are willing to accept alternative approaches to the study of human behavior that provide more understanding of human behavior than economics, should it not accept "common sense" and "direct experience"? Is there not implied in such a position the recognition of limitations of science? An important point in the foregoing discussion is that people can learn things as a part of interactive processes, like markets, that cannot be learned in any other way — by way of science, for example.

Those are the sorts of issues that have been raised by Frank Knight and others. Certainly, we may be able to learn *something* from the application of science to sexual behavior, but does it follow that from such an observation, the techniques of science can, *conceptually,* handle all dimensions of human sexuality? Indeed, there are good reasons for us to expect the penetration of *science* into this human dimension to be extremely limited.

Sexual behavior is an extraordinarily complicated *process* rather than an outcome, involving numerous variables, no combination of which is exactly the same for any two people. The variables involved are apparent to only the people involved in a given sexual experience. More importantly, the people involved may not know at any given point in the process *exactly* what it is they are pursuing. (They may have a generalized notion of what they are after, but empirical science requires a very specific objective function.) A sexual experience is largely a process of discovery; it is based on the actions and reactions of the parties involved — which can hardly be predicted beforehand. And the people involved in a given sexual act do not necessarily want the same thing, a conclusion that is hardly surprising when males and females are involved. Just because an outside observer-scientist sees two people go to bed in no way means that *very much* is known what the two "want" or even "are about to do." For this reason alone, the importance and usefulness of scientific analysis conducted by an outside observer must be highly suspect.

The problem confronting the extension of economics into nontraditional areas (especially interpersonal relationships) is that human relationships are a web of interactive processes in which the "goods" (or "wants" or "values") themselves are as much a part of the outcomes as the units consumed. More importantly, the "goods" are never quite the same to different people, and much of our uniquely human existence would be lost if they were.

As I noted in chapter 3, predictive (as opposed to abstract) scientific analysis of human behavior is founded upon the assumption that wants (values) and constraints are readily identifiable (observable). There must be constants, or predictability in science is a vacuous notion. Without constants we are unable to determine the "correctness" of the theory. Where wants are undefined or are defined *in the process* of behavior (and emerge slightly or substantially different each time a certain category of human interaction is experienced), it would appear that science has reached one of its limits. For science to be empirically valid, the X,s and Y's must be specified — exactly.

Now it may be true that a person in the middle of a heavily forested mountain range may, as Professor Watts suggests, devise some rational means of seeking out the highest peak in the range (or the peak with the "most attractive view," or whatever the goal may be) in the process of groping the way through the forest. Whether or not people attempt to be rational, or as rational as they can be, is not the issue. The issue is whether they can, at all times, be rational in their approach to confronting the external world (whether or not there must necessarily be a nonrational domain of behavior) and whether or not a scientific approach to understanding people's moves through the forest can be productive. If people devise what they consider to be a rational approach to solving goals that are only envisioned in the process of moving through the forest (or through a sexual experience), it would appear that a conceptual limit to science has been met.

Additionally, we must acknowledge that the "choosing" person is never quite the same, a point stressed by others.[6] Each choice is something important to the individual, something that changes his circumstances or "improves his lot." Each choice, in and of itself, may not alter the chooser in perceptible ways; but the stream of choices confronted by the chooser means that the individual is a constantly evolving person. This in turn means that not only are the X's and Y's not always the same, but the chooser cannot appraise the same X's or Y's in the same way, because he is not the same person. Does not such a circumstance limit the applicability of economic science?

Economics has had significant success in the analysis of market behavior because, in that sphere of human interaction, the goods are reasonably well defined by the trades. At least, economists can observe a part of what is at stake in this exchange relationship, and *the object of trades tends to dominate the relationship*. Those conditions are not nearly as well met in nonmarket human activity. Further, in analysis of nonmarket phenomena economists have tended to confine themselves to discussing "patterns of outcome" and not the "concrete content" of those patterns.

One great question confronting social science is how much of life is actually caught up in the problem of allocating efficiently scarce resources among competing and known wants. To the extent that, as Knight suggests, life is at bottom experimentation, the domain of predictive science must be conceptually limited. The practical limits of science must necessarily be established by "practice;" however, recognition of the existence of conceptual limits should help us see and appreciate the practical limits when they are reached.

Do not misunderstand what I am trying to say here. Of course, an investigator can count the number of times coitus takes place and the number of births that eventually occur. He may be able to predict, on the basis of his study, the number of times in a specified time period, under certain circumstances, people will engage in sexual intercourse. However, it is highly unlikely that he — as a social scientist — will have understood very much about the sexual dimensions of human behavior. Participants in processes do not always *count* exactly the way observers do, and, to that extent, the value of the observer's work will always be limited. It tends to follow that as economists move further and further away from well defined market transactions, criteria other than the predictability of the models will, of necessity, have to be employed in judging the worth of scientific inquiry. This is because the conceptual framework of neoclassical economics and its requirements of modeling and empirical verification will become progressively more suspect. As noted in the preceding chapters, what emerges is the problem of whether empirical analysis tests the correctness of a hypothesis or the appropriateness of a "proxy variable."

Free Will and Economic Science

Following in the footsteps of others, Professor Machan suggests that neoclassical economic theory is not necessarily grounded in the "creative" and "original" power of the subjective and that maintaining the contrary (as I do) is a misrepresentation of neoclassical economics. He tells us, "In the tradition of philosophical theories from within which neoclassical economic theory has emerged, the concept of free will does not to me appear to be widely accepted."[7]

If an original creative power is not implied by all the talk about the subjective in theory, I must wonder why the distinction has been made between constraints (which are presumed to be objective) and wants (which are presumed to be subjective). Why all the talk about "goods" and "bads," about the evaluation *by the individual?* Why is there a professional resistance to making interpersonal utility comparisons if there is not something highly individualized about evaluation?

Professor Machan adds that Austrian economists like von Mises and Hayek do not accept the concept of limited free will, a notion that appears to be implied in the concept of subjectivity. Machan points out that von Mises, for example, founded his analysis on the assumption that people are driven to eliminate some "uneasiness." That, Machan intimates, means that people do not have the capacity to originate actions. Such a conclusion is far from a correct interpretation of von Mises and Hayek. Both economists recognize that our capacity to originate action is limited — constrained within boundaries. From such an a priori contention, we can predict "patterns of outcomes." However, the "content" of the patterns is left open — to be filled in constrained but nondeterministic ways. Regardless of how individual values (or wants) are ultimately established (and all things are determined, either by some form of free choice or direction), an undeniable cornerstone of everything Hayek has written is our "constitutional ignorance" of those values.

The Limits of "as if"

Lastly, whenever neoclassical economics is attacked for unrealistic premises, a fallback position often taken is: Theory is based on the assumption that people behave "as if" they are rational. The sole criteria for evaluating theory are not involved with the question of whether or not they *are*, even to the remotest extent, rational, but whether or not the theory has predictive power. Although it appears that scientists would prefer to have a theory based on what "they" consider to be "realistic" assumptions rather than a theory whose assumptions are fully recognized as "unrealistic," the stated position has some merit — that is, when the theory generates hypotheses that can be empirically tested. However, not all theories can be empirically tested — which, contrary to protestations of strict positivists, does not necessarily make such theories completely useless. The necessary constants may not exist. As explained, such tends to be the case for theories of much (but certainly not all) nonmarket behavior. When empirically predictability breaks down (as it does in much, but not all, nonmarket behavior), it would appear that economists would be relatively more concerned about the "realism" (or a priori "truthfulness") of initial assumptions. When we theorize about behavior on an "as if" basis, not caring about the descriptive accuracy of the assumptions, we must have some external standard for the acceptance of the theory.

Notes

1. See two separate commentaries, "The Non-Rational Domain and the Limits of Economics: Comments" by Michael Watts and Tibor Machan, *Southern Economic Journal,* April 1981, pp. 1120–27; and the comments on "The Necessary Normative Context of Positive Economics" by Warren Samuels, *Journal of Economic Issues* 15, no 3 (September 1981): 721–27.
2. Watts, "Comments," p. 1121.
3. Machan, "Comments," p. 1123.
4. Ibid., p. 1124. For a source on Becker's views on the comparative usefulness of the economic approach, Machan cites a personal conversation he had with Becker at a 1978 Mount Pelerin Society meeting. He then offers in a footnote these comments:

Becker tells us that "In college I was attracted by the problems studied by sociologists and the analytic techniques used by economists" [*The Economic Approach,* p. 8]. Generally, the social sciences within the past half century have stressed the need for explanatory schemes. And "explanation" has generally meant, as used by social scientists, some type of causal/sequential account of events in human affairs, one which serves to identify factors (dependent and independent variables) that produce certain events of interest to us. This conception of what it is to explain and understand human affairs is not at all uncontroversial, open to not negligible challenge. The mere response to it from many social scientists is that it is at least useful to look at things that way, but "useful" seems to cash out into something that is problematic in itself. [A.R. Louch, *Explanation and Human Action* (Berkeley: University of California Press, 1976); Tibor R. Machan, *The Pseudo-Science of B.F. Skinner* (New Rochelle, N.Y.: Arlington House, 1974); Alexander Rosenberg, *Microeconomic Laws: A Philosophical Approach* (Pittsburgh: University of Pittsburgh Press, 1976); and Alexander Rosenberg, "Can Economic Theory Explain Everything?" *Philosophy of the Social Sciences,* December 1979, pp. 509–29.]

5. Professor Machan writes:

Is the assumption that "people are rational" as understood by Becker adequately explicated by saying, as does McKenzie: "People know what they want, are able to order their wants from most preferred to least preferred, and are able to act consistently on the basis of that ordering so as to maximize some general welfare notion such as utility, which Becker often calls 'full income.'" The term "able" is crucial here. For people may well be *able* to do what Becker supposedly considers vital to being rational amounts to, and yet they may not be *willing* to do it. I suspect that Becker's, like other economists, conception of rationality is committed to the view that rational people *will* order their wants, etc., and *will* act consistently, etc. A mere capacity, such as the ability to order wants and the ability to act consistently, is unlikely to give to economists what it appears they demand of an adequate economic science, namely, the analytic tools for making predictions. From my ability to play tennis it does not follow, even if I have the knowledge of what I want and the opportunity to play tennis, that I *will* play tennis. ["Comments," p. 1124]

6. James M. Buchanan, *The Reason for Rules* (Cambridge: Cambridge University Press, forthcoming).
7. Machan, "Comments," p. 1125.

APPENDIX: THE LIMITATIONS OF SCIENTIFIC METHOD IN ECONOMICS

Frank H. Knight

The Meaning of Science

Since economics deals with human beings, the problems of its scientific treatement involves fundamental problems of the relations between man and his world. From a rational or scientific point of view, all practically real problems are problems in economics. The problem of life is to utilize resources "economically," to make them go as far as possible in the production of desired results. The general theory of economics is therefore simply the rationale of life. — In so far as it has any rationale! The first question in regard to scientific economics is this question of how far life is rational, how far its problems reduce to the form of using given means to achieve given ends. Now this, we shall contend, is not very far; the scientific view of life is a limited and partial view; life is at bottom an exploration in the field of values, an attempt to discover values, rather than on the basis of knowledge of them to produce and enjoy them to the greatest possible extent. We strive to "know ourselves," to find out our real wants, more than to get what we want. This fact sets a first and most sweeping limitation to the conception of economics as a science.

Even this statement of the scientific view of life as the conscious utilization of resources for given ends involves stretching the term scientific as compared with

Condensed and reprinted, with permission of Mrs. Ethel Knight, from Frank H. Knight, *The Ethics of Competition* (Chicago: University of Chicago Press, 1976), pp. 105–147, which in turn reprinted the article from *The Trend of Economics,* edited by Rexford G. Tugwell, by permission of F.S. Crofts and Company, Publishers.

its most exact signification. It involves conceding the reality and potency of conscious thinking and planning, which in the narrowest meaning of science are illusory. From a *rigorously* scientific viewpoint, life is a mere matter of mechanics; what human beings think of as practical problems of conduct are subjective illusions; thinking and planning and all subjectivity are illusions; human actions are a detail in a cosmic panorama of the transformation of motion. But since it is impossible to discuss value in purely objective terms, we must simply assume the reality of the conscious data and leave it to philosophy to reconcile the contradiction, or to decide that it cannot be reconciled. We have to accept the common-sense notion of value or worth as our starting-point.

Two sorts of experience are recognized as having worth, or as capable of having it — an active and a passive; one is creation or control, and the other appreciation. These are not strictly separate experiences, but rather "aspects" of experience, yet they are practically separable to a large degree. The worth of active creation or control is a kind of appreciation; usually, the worth of the experience of activity depends more or less upon a feeling of worth toward or appreciation of some "result" brought about. But though the two things are usually more or less associated and overlapping, we are all familiar with extreme cases in which on the one hand the feeling of worth is nearly or quite purely passive and on the other the worth of an activity is nearly or quite independent of the character of the result. The literature of value, like that of science, shows a bias for monism, so there is a tendency to reduce all value to "contemplation" or to the "joy of being a cause," according to the temperamental predilections of the particular writer, but a candid observer must accept both, and all sorts of mixtures of the two.

Each of these fundamental categories also exhibits two sub-types. In the case of appreciation we distinguish an effective or emotional or aesthetic, and a cognitive or intellectual pleasure. The mixtures and interrelations of these are again complex, but again we do separate, more or less, a worth which is pure appreciation from a worth which is a matter of "understanding." We do care to understand things which we feel to be repulsive, and we do care for things which we feel no impulse to try to understand. Sometimes the one sort of worth contributes to the other, and sometimes they appear to conflict. The aesthetic experience of the cultivated person is in part a matter of understanding how a painting, say, or a piece of music or poem produces its effect, but also the aesthetic experience may be endangered by too much analysis. In general, it appears that beauty must involve a certain amount of illusion; the "machinery" must not be too manifest, or the interest in it too strong, or the effect is lost.

In the field of activity, also, there is a separation, less easy to make clearly, between that which is *spontaneous,* going to its end directly and immediately, and that which involves a conscious, calculated marshalling of means. The distinction holds for both the activity whose worth is inherent and that whose worth lies rather in the result which it produces. In creation and control as in appreciation, there is more or less conflict between understanding and enjoying. We strive to understand the how and why of our actions, to analyze the technique; and yet when this process is carried too far, and it becomes altogether a matter of routine manipulation of means to produce an effect preconceived and foreseen, there is a loss of interest in the action. It might be interesting, if space allowed, to go into the problem of classifying our value experiences on the basis of the various combinations of these types, but our purpose is merely to sketch certain aspects of the meaning of science in connection with the field of values.

The immediate purpose of science is to enable us to *understand,* which again covers the understanding both of beauty and of the technique of action. But our modern, sophisticated way of thinking tends more and more to subordinate the desire for understanding as such to a desire for control. It can hardly be doubted that the spirit of science itself makes for this interpretation. A scientific age tends to relegate understanding for its own sake to the realm of sentiment and romance, an order of value regarded rather contemptuously in comparison with considerations or practice and power. The value of science is found in the *results* which make it possible to achieve, and science itself takes its place as a tool, tending toward the level of necessary evils. The love of science is brought by the scientific spirit into the position of a sentiment to be viewed apologetically. In the scientific, evolutionary, view of the world, too, the scientific interest is "explained" as a Spencerian transfer of attention from the real end to the means, which becomes erected into a pseudo-end.

Some rather obvious restrictions in outlook which arise from giving too predominant a place to science may be mentioned at this point. A scientific atmosphere obscures if it does not eclipse a considerable part of the field of values. It centers attention on the results of activity, weakening or destroying the value of the process. In addition, it emphasizes the quantitative aspect of the result which can be treated scientifically as against the qualitative or aesthetic aspect which cannot. For these reasons activity comes to be concentrated along lines where results can be predicted and brought about "efficiently," that is, in the largest possible quantity with relation to a given stock of resources or productive power. This means concentration in lines of essentially repetitious work as contrasted with the spontaneous and creative. For science, manifestly, cannot direct creation in any true sense; it can only copy, or at best rearrange old elements in new combinations. True creation, which is the field of art, involves the invention of new ends as well as new means for reaching them. Science is always striving to "understand" art and produce its effects by the calculated application of rules; but to the extent that it succeeds in its endeavor the result is no longer art in the true sense. The evil is multiplied by the fact that because science can never explain why this is so, it tends to deny the fact. Real creation involves a very different technique; or, it is better to say, it is not a matter of technique at all, but a kind of psychic sympathy or entering of the mind of the artist into his medium and a handling of it from the inside, whereas science works externally. Yet the contradiction already referred to is conspicuous here. The artist needs a great deal of scientific knowledge and technique; but when his work becomes reduced to these terms it ceases to be art and becomes merely copy-work . . .

But to proceed with the definition of science: From the standpoint of knowledge, the problem of control is a problem of *prediction*. Conduct, which is the adaptation of means to ends, is necessarily forward-looking. To behave intelligently means to act in the light of valid knowledge as to what would happen in the given situation in the absence of interference from myself, and of the changes in this course of events which will result from any contemplated action of mine. In case I cannot bring about any change in the natural progress of events, or at least not any desirable change, I must still be able to foresee the progress itself, in order to react intelligently toward it. From the standpoint of a strict view of conscious behavior, we are not interested in the world as it is, except as a basis of predicting what it will be in the immediate or remote future to which conscious plans of action relate.

Science, then, is merely the *technique of prediction*. It is the mental mechanism or process by means of which we act intelligently. From the scientific standpoint (or this quasi-scientific view which accepts motives as real causes) to "live" intelligently and to "act" intelligently are interchangeable expressions. And to act "intelligently" (shifting the emphasis) means to act in such a way as to bring about the result foreseen and intended; it goes without saying that any result brought about by deliberate action is a desired result. It is important to keep in mind that not all control is scientific in the sense of involving conscious, deliberate adaptation of means to the production of desired ends. Control begins in the control of our own bodies, since it is only upon them that mind or purpose can act directly. It is questionable how far this control of our muscular system is ever "scientific" at any stage, and it is certain that it tends strongly to become unconscious and automatic, reverting to our second type of control experience noted above. Such fundamental activities as speech, for example, are probably learned in the first place by a process of trial-and-error or by accident involving little conscious adaptation. A good part of it is no doubt "instinctive," such as the modulation of the voice to convey emotion. Any skilled technique when well learned drops largely below the threshold. A trained pianist or typist thinks as little about the keys he strikes as does any normal person about the position of his vocal organs in articulation, and the skilled mechanic uses his tools in much the same automatic way; they have in effect become a part of his body. Perhaps the military strategist too may come to manipulate his army with little more thought than the skilled driver of a motor car gives to his pedals and controls . . .

The Technique of Prediction, or the Logic of Science

All science may be regarded as an elaboration and refinement of the principle that we judge the future by the past. A scientific treatment of the problem of prediction and control must assume that this is just as true whether the process is one of conscious or unconscious knowledge, deliberate or automatic response. Even if man, like the lower animals, inherits adaptive reaction patterns, the basis of the adaptation is the same. A scientific world view has no possible place for the intuitive, or any other foresight of *new* truth, in advance of perception. Its fundamental assumption is that *truth is always the same* and is known through perception and memory. But that truth is always the same is equivalent to saying that the world is always the same. Change is unreal, or in so far as there is real change, the world is knowable only historically, the future is unpredictable.

The paradox, that if the world is always the same there is no problem of prediction, while if it is not always the same prediction is impossible, is resolved by means of two fundamental notions, law, and rearrangement, or analysis-synthesis. The essential idea in law is change of an interchanging character, that a thing does not change in "essence" if it changes predictably, since it remains true to its nature which is to change in the same unchanging way. Any predictable change, and any that science can discuss, is therefore analogous to movement along a path which can be represented by an equation, and of which any part can be calculated from the formula for any other part, however small.

The conceptual hiatus between a static and a changing world is further bridged in another way by the idea of rearrangement of the same elements in different combinations. Ultimately, both of these ideas merge in laws of rearrangement in the literal sense of spatial movement. Science refuses to credit the idea of internal, independent changes in simple elementary things, even in accordance with law, and insists on reducing all change to changes in the relations of unchanging elements or units. So the ordinary objects of experience are split up hypothetically into elements in terms of whose rearrangements are explained those changes in sensible things which are not brought into correspondence with external changes. A complete scientific explanation of the world would leave nothing but actual, literal motion. Of course the idea of such an explanation cannot be taken very seriously. The human mind balks at the outset at the notion of movement without something that moves, and the logical process of reducing change to motion attenuates the moving particles into a form imperceptible to sense and unreal to imagination. Moreover, practically speaking, mechanics itself has never been able to get along without the notion of force, which is quite clearly a mode of consciousness and not an existence perceived in the outside world. For practical purposes, again, we must stop far short of the ideal of rigorous scientific conceptions, and survey the process by which our minds organize that sort of provisional knowledge on which conduct is based (outside of scientific laboratories, and in large part within them also).

To begin with, consciousness organizes the "big, buzzing, booming confusion," which is experience in its raw state, into a world of objects, existing and moving and changing in space and time. Our behavior is concerned with the properties of *things,* including their modes of behavior, which are truly properties as much as are the sense qualities. Properties and modes of behavior of things form the content of knowledge and the subject-matter of thought as the basis of action.[1] The axiom at the basis of practical thinking, the principle of identity or static principle already referred to, is simply that things remain "essentially" the same, that they have an inner nature which does not change. They may change as far as sensible properties are concerned, but only according to unchanging "law" and in definite relation to other things. We may state this axiom simply in the proposition that the same thing will behave in the same way under the same circumstances. The idea of a "thing," or identity itself, is just the recognition of permanence or sameness in the organization of qualities, as is clearly shown by what happens in reasoning.

If behavior meant only dealing with "the same things in the same circumstances," in a literal sense, there would be no occasion for thinking as we use the term. Intelligence would be a matter of *mere* memory. But the variety of things with which we have to deal is indefinitely too great for our minds to become acquainted with them; they do not remain the same in the perceptual sense, and the "circumstances" (which means their relations to other things) are similarly complicated and variable. These two facts, the mentally unmanageable complexity of manifoldness of the things which make up our world, and their habit of apparent change, necessitate the activity of thinking. In this sketch we shall not go into the logic of atomism by which sensible change is supposed to be reduced to rearrangement in space, and which belongs more to philosophy than to the logic of practice. Our study will concern itself only with the manner of formulation of those factual laws of change by means of which it is possible to predict the future and to behave intelligently . . .

Two introductory sections have aimed to clarify the meaning of science as a technique of prediction, and the conditions requisite to scientific prediction in any field of data. These conditions may be regarded as a part of the definition of science. Knowledge usable for prediction in the guidance of conduct must consist of propositions which state unchanging truth and hence can be made only with regard to data which are ultimately static. Merely historic facts are of no direct practical use, and it would conduce to clear thinking to separate sharply scientific from historical truth in the terminology. In general, a scientific proposition must hold good for a class of objects or situations; it states a dependable association or a numerical probability of an association between an attribute not open to direct observation and one which is so, and usually expresses a quantitative relation between the two. In general, truth cannot be considered scientific unless it is demonstrable, which means that it must be alike for all observers and accurately communicable. The scientific view of experience postulates a world which is independent of observation, and hence is of course really the same for all observers. But it is to be noted that there can be no scientific evidence for this view beyond the actual tendency of observers to agree. There is in fact the widest divergence in the amount of agreement among different observations according to the character of the data. There is never any close agreement quantitatively, but science has in many fields evolved a technique of *measurement* which compels agreement. In the field of human attributes and behavior, all these prerequisites — the stability of the data, their assimilability into classes, even their objectivity and especially the possibility of their objective measurement — will be found subject to sweeping limitations which set corresponding limits to the scientific treatment of the phenomena.

The Scientific Treatment of Human Data

A very large portion of the conduct of any human being is related in some way to other human beings, and if it is to be intelligent, it must be based upon correct prediction of their behavior; and, needless to say, we desire and need the power of controlling the behavior of persons quite as commonly as in the case of other phases of the "environment." It goes without saying that we do predict more or less correctly in this field, and act more or less intelligently in relation to other persons. We know what to expect of them under various circumstances, we count upon them in innumerable ways without being disappointed in the outcome in anything approaching the proportion of cases called for by the law of probability if our predictions were unfounded. And we do influence the conduct of others by deliberate action. But does this unquestioned fact or prediction and control by common-sense methods prove the possibility of scientific treatment? The question is whether it is possible to *improve upon the performance of common sense,* as science has done in the realm of physics and biology, by the conscious formulation and use of rules based upon a wider comparison and more careful analysis of cases.

At the outset we are confronted with a problem as to what *is* the method of common sense in predicting human behavior, and what the correct relation to it of the method of science. It is fairly clear that common sense does not reach its conclusions in this field by comparing and analyzing cases as objective phenomena, treating human beings as "things," and observing their uniformities. It *connects actions with feelings* and pictures behavior in the closest association with, if not by means of, an idea of the *conscious attitude* of the other person. The behavior attributes of human beings constitute character or personality, which is thought of in a quite different way from such physical qualities as the fluidity of water or the explosiveness of dynamite. Should science proceed in the same way, and associate feelings with situations and actions with feelings, or should it establish its relations between situations and actions directly?

The latter seems the simpler course, and the youngest of the sciences, calling itself Behaviorism, has arisen to advocate this method of procedure. The behaviorist points out that primitive man attributes consciousness to inanimate objects just as we attribute it to ourselves and our fellow beings, and contends that we should grow out of the childish practice in the one case as we have in the other. There is no way of demonstrating whether any reaction is conscious or not, or what sort of consciousness if any accompanies it, not to mention the problem of finding where in the evolutionary scale consciousness appears. It is a plausible inference that the proper procedure is to ignore consciousess and infer the responses of human beings to situations from previous observation and analysis of their responses to situations. The behaviorist (in the exuberance of his enthusiasm) is likely to go further and deny outright that consciousness actually has anything to do with behavior or that there is any such thing. But in this he is turning philosopher and carrying the discussion outside the field of science. The practical questions is whether the notion of consciousness is *useful* in prediction. It might indeed be just as useful if consciousness did not ''really exist'' as if it did, and it is the usefulness, not the existence, which practically concerns us. Scientific discussion does not always keep science separate from metaphysics as it should do.

It is impossible to argue at length in this paper the issues involved in behaviorism; we can only state briefly our own position, which is that consciousness *is* useful, and its recognition necessary and inevitable, in the interpretation of human behavior. The reason is simply that we cannot help ourselves. (And it may be admissible to step over into the domain of the metaphysical problem long enough to note that the same reasoning justifies accepting the ontological reality of consciousness, that it is the only sort of reason we ever have for believing in the existence of anything.) As a matter of fact we never succeed entirely in eliminating consciousness from our ideas of material things. We have noted that mechanics has not been able to do without the notion of force, though whatever force is, more than motion, is a fact of consciousness. It is impossible to construct in thought a world of real objects in purely objective terms; if objects are to have the qualities of consistent behavior they are inevitably thought of as possessing rudiments of mind. We interpret the behavior of the most material thing by to some degree putting ourselves in its place. Still more true is this when we come to consider the behavior of living things. Purely mechanical biology remains an aspiration of the scientific intellect. Some sort of teleology is inevitable in speaking of the phenomena of life. The *will* to live and to increase is more than the *fact* of living and increasing, and we cannot account satisfactorily to ourselves for the facts of the lowest animal and plant life without recognizing an *element of striving* as well as processes and results.

In the field of human behavior we have indefinitely stronger reasons for accepting consciousness as real and potent, in the fact of *communication*. The conclusive reason for believing that an action is conscious is that the subject can *tell us so,* and tell us about the motives. Logically, the behaviorist is right; we do not perceive consciousness, in any other person at least; we cannot prove or verify it; we only infer it from behavior. But in spite of logic we all recognize that as a matter of fact we know consciousness more surely and positively than we know the behavior from which theoretically we infer it. We cannot scientifically explain, except most superficially, how we communicate feelings or read expression in the looks and acts and words of others. Yet if anything in human life is clear it is that our whole intellectual life is built upon the fact of communication. Without it we could never develop the idea of objectivity, the foundation of scientific reasoning, and as noted in the preceding section, the test of reality is the possibility of verification, which depends on communication with the consciousness of others.

If the objective cannot exist without intercommunication, it is a truism that the subjective cannot be discussed without it. There is a mystery about our being able to talk and understand each other in regard to purely subjective experiences, but there is no question of the fact. It would appear, especially in view of the fact that we have no knowledge of purely objective reality, that we must concede some sort of consciousness to anything that can be made a subject of intelligent discourse. In connection with the problem of conduct it is surely clear that if consciousness is denied and a behavioristic position assumed, an end is put at once to the possibility of discussing values or motives. We might discuss activity — though it is not easy to see how the discussion could have any "meaning" — and even the "cause" of activity (in the phenomenalistic use of the word), but there would be no such thing as a "reason" for activity; the idea of reasons would become meaningless and the subject-matter of all discussion of values unreal.

How do these considerations affect the possibility of scientific prediction of conduct? Within limits, it is possible to discover laws of behavior, as such, in the objective sense. The term "man" denotes a very real and distinct class of "object;" seldom is there disagreement as to whether any particular specimen belongs to the class. And yet, outside of physiological processes and reflexes (and even these are not at all uniform) it is astonishingly hard to find traits or characteristic definite reactions which one can confidently infer from membership in the class, which are common to substantially all members of it. Even laughing, crying, and talking are not definite reactions to definite stimuli. In this field the "laws" which we may hope to reach are at best statistical in character, and even these are subject to narrow limitations, for reasons which will be pointed out presently.

The behavior of human beings depends upon their *previous history*, and the history of no two individuals is the same or closely similar, *in essential respects*. The difficulty is that the reactions assuming them, to be determinate, are affected *in a large degree* by *imperceptible* differences in the situation. This is illustrated by the stories of "clever" animals. Dogs and horses have frequently seemed to their trainers to be reacting to spoken commands, but careful experiment has shown that this was not true at all, that they were really dependent upon some "cue" involuntarily and unconsciously given by the trainer himself and so subtle in character that careful study has sometimes failed to disclose just what it was. The wide divergence in the results obtained by different persons attempting to influence people *by the same technique* is a familiar fact, as also that the effects of laws and administrative measures seldom correspond to the expectations of their framers. Even in the case of the elemental and "gross" motives this is true. Who can say whether a specified punishment will reduce a particular crime? Whether dropping bombs on any enemy population will weaken or strengthen their military morale? Whether raising wages will cause men to work harder or to loaf, or what the effect of a change in the price of diamonds will be upon the sales? It depends! . . .

To repeat, it is possible for a good judge of human nature to form opinions with a high degree of validity as to what individuals or groups are likely to do under conditions present to observation. Moreover, it is possible to convey information and describe situations intelligibly to a considerable extent, and to make general statements regarding the art of judging human nature which have some degree of helpfulness. But none of this is done by the methods of science. It is all in the field of art, and not of science, of suggestion and interpretation, and not accurate, definite, objective statement, a sphere in which common sense works and logic falls down, and where, in consequence, the way to improve our technique is not to attempt to analyze things into their elements, reduce them to measure and determine functional relations, but to educate and train our intuitive powers . . .

The kind of thing which human nature is is shown by the forms of language used in describing it. Discussion of human nature, like discussion of art works, runs to a relatively slight extent in terms of objective, sensible qualities, but predominantly in language which suggests rather than asserts; its meanings are conveyed by figurative rather than literal forms of expression. It is difficult to appreciate the relative importance of figurative language as compared with literal. By far the greater part of written and spoken discourse is more or less figurative, and it not only conveys a meaning, but usually a meaning which it would be impossible to express directly, scientifically. People are far more concerned with meanings than with sense qualities, and meaning, being a subjective phenomenon, must be suggested rather than stated. The behaviorist-materialist may insist that expressions like "a stalwart soul," and "my love's like a red, red rose" are "really" based on physical similarity of some attenuated sort. But he cannot point out in terms of sense qualities wherein the resemblance consists, and his assertion is therefore mere dogma, as far from the "facts" of experience as the ravings of any mystic. One is just as free to believe that there is more to it than physical resemblance in any sense, that there is a realm of meanings no less real than the verifiable world of physics. It is doubtful whether any language except possibly the arbitrary symbols of mathematics and symbolic logic, is entirely literal, just as is seems that reality cannot be thought of in purely objective terms. The meanings which are conveyed, but not expressed, by figurative language, cannot be taken apart and put together, and it is a misuse of the term "analysis" to apply it to our thought concerning them, just as all the rest of the technique of natural science is misapplied in their sphere.

Economics as a Science

In spite of all the foregoing, there is a science of economics, a true, and even exact, science, which reaches laws as universal as those of mathematics and mechanics. The greatest need for the development of economics as a growing body of thought and practice is an adequate appreciation of the meaning, and the limitations, of this body of accurate premises and rigorously established conclusions. It comes about in the same general way as all science, except perhaps in a higher degree, i.e., through abstraction. There are no laws regarding the *content* of economic behavior, but there are laws universally valid as to its *form*. There is an abstract rationale of all conduct which is rational at all, and a rationale of all social relations arising through the organization of rational activity. We cannot tell what particular goods any person will desire, but we can be sure that within limits he will prefer more of any good to less, and that there will be limits beyond which the opposite will be true. We do not know what specific things will be wealth at any given place and time, but we know quite well what must be the attitude of any sane individual toward wealth wherever a social situation exists which gives the concept meaning. In the same way we know that in any productive operations on this earth there are some general relations between quantity of resources used and quantity of product turned out.

These principles are only less abstract than those of mathematics. It is never true in reality that two and two make four; for we cannot add unlike things and there are no two real things in the universe which are exactly alike. It is only to completely abstract units, entirely without content, that the most familiar laws of number and quantity apply. Yet no one questions the practical utility of such laws. They are infinitely more useful than they could be if they ever did fit exactly any single concrete base, since all that they lose in literal accuracy they gain in generality of application. By not being strictly true in any case they are significantly true in all.

It is not necessary to regard the general, *a priori* laws of mathematics or economics or such mechanical principles as inertia as being "intuitively" known in any inscrutable way. They may all be more advantageously treated as mere facts of observation, characteristics of the world we live in, but characteristics so obvious that it is impossible to escape recognizing them and so fundamental that to think them away would necessitate creating in the imagination a different type of universe. The "necessary" character of axioms is undoubtedly due, not to their being created or given to experience by mind, but rather on the contrary to the fact that the mind has not the creative power to imagine a world fundamentally different from that in which we actually live.

This conception readily fits the character of the general laws of economic theory, such as diminishing utility and diminishing returns. The former is a general statement of the *fact* that men with a given quantity of exchange power do not (unless they are feeble-minded) expend it all upon the first commodity they run across, or the one which happens to be uppermost in mind at the moment, but distribute it in some more or less determinate way over the available goods. There *is* a valid distinction between the intelligent and stupid or insane expenditure of money.

In the same way there is, and every normal adult *knows* that there is, a general law of the relation between quantity of resources expended and quantity of goods produced. It is a fact of the world we live in that "goods" are usually produced, not by single agencies working alone but by a combination of resources, in much the same way that "satisfaction" is produced by consuming a variety of goods; and the character of the dependence is much the same in the two cases. In a universe governed by a general law of increasing returns the output of goods would be increased by decreasing the amount of resources devoted to their production. Such a universe would be bedlam.

It is a common objection to deductive economic theory that from obvious principles only obvious conclusions can be established and nothing really significant can come of it. This assertion is belied by the facts of economic science itself, not to mention mathematics, where a structure of boundless and ever-growing scope and intricacy is built up on the basis of a few simple axioms. Yet it all "works;" its conclusions are descriptive of reality and are indispensable in predicting and controlling the phenomena of the physical world. In economics also, the significance of the conclusions of general theory is patent. They are not "obvious," since the ablest students are not in agreement in regard to many of them, nor useless for practical purposes, since the broad outlines of social policy depend upon them and are quite commonly misguided through the failure of legislators and administrators to understand and follow them.

Nor are the general laws of economics "institutional." They work in an institutional setting, and upon institutional material; institutions supply much of their content and furnish the machinery by which they work themselves out, more or less quickly and completely, in different actual situations. Institutions may determine the alternatives of choice and fix the limits of freedom of choice, but the general laws of choice among competing motives or goods are not institutional — unless rational thinking and an objective world are institutions, an interpretation which would make the term meaningless. Economic activity consists in the use of certain resources by certain processes, to produce "wealth." The content of the concept wealth is largely institutional, and the resources available and processes known and used at any place and time for producing wealth are in a sense historical products; but there are general laws of production and consumption which hold good whatever specific things are thought of as wealth and whatever productive factors and processes in use.

For illustration we may consider the assertion commonly made even by economists who do not recognize the function of general laws, that the way to understand price fixation is to study the machinery and process of marketing. The mode of organization of the market may indeed have a good deal to do with price, and that in at least two ways. It brings the buyers and sellers of the goods more or less perfectly into communication with each other, furnishing the channels through which the real price-fixing forces, the facts of demand and supply, work out more or less freely and effectively to a determinate result. In addition, what we call marketing machinery and organization includes a large element of direction of energy into manipulation of demand, creating real or fictitious qualities in the goods marketed, through true or false information, or through mere psychological compulsion in the form of suggestion and exhortation. In so far as these things are present and operative, they are, of course present and operative; but they do not affect the fact that in the large the conditions of supply and demand determine the prices of goods. Other considerations produce aberrations from the result of perfect intercommunication among buyers and sellers who know the goods and their wants, but they are to be understood only as producing *aberrations from* the fundamental tendency and hence in subordination to it. They are of the nature of friction, divergence of materials from conditions taken as standard, and the like, in the workings of the laws of mechanics in actual machines.

There is a close analogy between theoretical economics and theoretical physics. Both treat of the relations between cause and effect, between force and change, without reference to the question of what forces may actually be at work in any particular case or what effects it may be desirable to produce. In both fields, the *application* of the principles does depend precisely upon these questions of the particular ends in view and means at hand, and upon all the conditions present. But the application of principles is impossible without principles to apply. It is no argument against the practical value of pure theory that taken alone it does not yield definite rules for guidance. It is a recognized fact that laboratory physics could not have made anything approximating its actual progress in modern times without the aid of a relatively separate development of mathematical theory by men who have not been experimenters.

The laws of economics are never themselves institutional, though they may relate to institutional situations. Some, as we have observed, are as universal as rational behavior, the presence of alternatives of choice between quantitatively variable ends, or between different means of arriving at ends. Others are as universal as "organized activity," independent of the form or method of organization. A large part of the extant body of economic theory would be as valid in a socialistic society as it is in one organized through exchange between individuals. Other laws relate to behavior in exchange relations, and of course have no practical significance where such relations are not established. Still others cover behavior in situations created by even more special institutional arrangements, as for example the differences in business conduct created by the custom of selling goods subject to cash discount or by the existence of a branch banking system as contrasted with independent banks. An intelligent conception of the meaning of science requires a clear grasp of the meaning of classification and subclassification, of laws of all degrees of generality. Each law is universal in the field to which it applies, though it may not give a complete description of the cases which it fits. Quite commonly a law has the form *"in so far as* the situation is of such a character, such things will happen."* Any law is significant if it gives a sufficient part of the explanation of a sufficiently common type of occurrence.

Scientific laws fall into a sort of hierarchical order from still another point of view than that of the classes of phenomena to which they apply. A law states that under given conditions given changes will occur. But the "given conditions" may be only relatively given, and may themselves be changing in relation to other causes which condition them, and so on. After explaining an event in terms of causes immediately at work, it may be necessary to explain those causes, bringing in other causes to be explained in turn. To a large extent these stages in the process of explanation fall in different sciences, one taking as data the results of another; but sometimes several stages may fall within the province of one science. The latter is true in economics, and the problem of what are to be treated as data becomes especially troublesome. We shall return to this point shortly.

If the term economics were to be interpreted in the literal sense, as covering all behavior which involves the adaptation of means to ends and the "economizing" of means in order to maximize ends, then economics would be an almost all-inclusive science. It would take in about all of what we call rational behavior, since thinking is just the technique for guiding the performance of this function. But the study of this vast field falls into certain natural divisions, and after all the generations of discussion there is still need for clear delimitation of these and recognition of the methods appropriate to each. The process of want-satisfaction, or rational behavior, involves certain elementary factors: (1) the wants to be satisfied, (2) the goods, uses or services of goods, and human services, which satisfy them, (3) intermediate goods in a complicated sequence back to (4) ultimate resources, on which the production of goods depends, (5) a series of technological processes of conversion, and (6) a human organization for carrying out these processes. This human organization again is two-fold, including (6–a) the internal organization of productive units or enterprises, which belongs rather to the field of technology than to that of the other phase which is (6–b) the social organization of production and distribution in the large. Theoretical economics as the term is generally used is concerned almost exclusively with the very last factor, the general social organization, in which the nation and to a large extent the world is the unit.

As a basis of division of labor in the investigation and study of a field which is still vastly too broad for a single science, it is tacitly agreed to separate further certain *methods* of organization as fields for different groups of workers. The most important division is that between *political organization,* on the one hand, covering the various methods such as monarchy, democracy, etc., based on territorial sovereignty, and on the other hand what has come to be called *the* economic organization, worked out through exchange in markets and prices of goods and services. Thus economic theory has in practice come to be restricted to the analysis of social interaction and coordination through the price mechanism, that is, of organization through the competitive sale for money by individuals (really by families) of productive services (of person and "property") to business enterprises, and the competitive purchase from business enterprises with the money obtained of goods for consumption. It is the business enterprise, variously constituted, which carries on the actual production. Thus of the three main elements in economic life, wants resources, and organization, economy theory deals directly with one aspect of the organization, and only incidentally with the other elements. Wants are in the province of psychology, sociology, and ethics; resources fall in various other sciences, and the technological aspects of organization to a vast number, and the internal organization of business to a special branch of economics.

The great fact which makes economic theory so vague and so difficult is the confusion already referred to as to the relations between cause and effect or the interpretation of "given" conditions, or in scientific terms, the separation of the constants and independent variables, from the dependent variables. This problem underlies the crude distinction often drawn between "static" and "dynamic" economics, and between short-time and long-time views of the price problem. It is also central to the issue between the conceptions of economics as deductive theory and as "institutional" economics. All these contrasted notions are purely relative, matters of degree; at one extreme we might have a discussion limited to the abstract theory of markets, at which point indeed some of the mathematical treatments virtually stop; at the other extreme we should have the philosophy of history (in the economic field, however defined) and that is what institutional economics practically comes to. It should go without saying that all are useful and necessary.

To begin with, needless confusion has been caused by the unfortunate use of the terms "static" and "dynamic." These are highly objectionable because they have in mechanics a definite meaning unrelated to the main issue in economics. The problem of conditions of equilibrium among given forces — "statics" in the proper sense — is often important in economics, but is after all subsidiary, as indeed it is in physical mechanics. The larger question is that of whether the forces acting under given conditions tend to produce an equilibrium, and if so how, and if not what is their tendency; that is, it is a problem in dynamics. This type of problem has been too largely passed over hitherto, leaving a fatal gap in the science. The crying need of economic theory to-day is for a study of the "laws of motion," the *kinetics* of economic changes. Physics could hardly have made a start until two sorts of resistance to change were sharply distinguished, that is, inertia and friction. The centering of economic theory about the possibility and condition of equilibrium has caused the study of the laws governing economic changes in time to be neglected. The least serious attempt to formulate and use the concepts of mass, momentum, energy, etc., or their analogues, in relation to economic change, and to measure force and acceleration, would have shed a flood of light on the contrast between mechanics and economics and the methodologies of study in the two fields.

We can hardly over-emphasize the contrast between economic dynamics in this proper sense — the study of the laws of change under given conditions — and the major problem above indicate, as to what conditions are to be treated as given. At the very outset we are confronted with a question in regard to which confusion reigns supreme, the question whether and in what sense human wants are to be considered in economics as data (or independent variables). We are not called upon to argue this question here, but merely to point out that it is by no means simply answered. Wants are usually treated as *the* fundamental data, the ultimate driving force in economic activity, and in a short-run view of problems this is scientifically legitimate.[2] But in the long-run it is just as clear that wants are dependent variables, that they are largely caused and formed by economic activity. The case is somewhat like that of a river and its channel; for the time being the channel locates the river, but in the long-run it is the other way.

Similar statements hold for the other half-dozen elements in the economic problem. The means of want-satisfaction and the resources used to produce them, and the technology and business organization according to which the process is carried out — all are *data,* causes, independent variables, in some regards and with reference to some time periods, and all are effects, dependent variables, in other regards and with reference to other time periods. The only ultimately independent variables are those features of nature and human nature which are in fact outside the power of economic forces to change, and it would be hard to say what these are. Even the laws of technology and physiology operate in economic relations as people believe them to be rather than as they are, and our beliefs concerning them are by no means fixed or independent of economic events.

Such a mass of interrelated data seems to call for a combination of three methods of treatment which must logically be sharply differentiated. The first is economic theory in the recognized sense, a study, largely deductive in character, of the more general aspects of economic cause and effect, those tendencies of a price system which are independent of the specific wants, technology, and resources. The second division, or applied economics, should attempt a statistical and inductive study of the actual data at the particular place and time, and of the manner in which general laws are modified by special and accidental circumstances of all sorts. That is, on the one hand it should get the facts as to the wants, resources, and technology in the situation to which the study is intended to apply, and the precise form of such functional relations as the general theory cannot describe more accurately than to say for example that they are "decreasing;" and in the second place it should ascertain and take account of facts and principles too special in character for the general theory, or which are not matters of general agreement. The argument of the third section of this paper should prove that this branch of the science is subject to very narrow limitations; the data lack the stability, classifiability, and measurability requisite to scientific treatment, and actual economic practice must as we have argued be at least as much an art based on wide general knowledge and sound judgment as a science with accurate premises and rigorous conclusions.

The third division of economics is the philosophy of history in the economic field, or what some of its votaries have chosen to call "historical" and others "institutional" economics, studying "the cumulative changes of institutions." In so far as it aspires to practical utility it will endeavor to predict long-period changes in the factors which applied economics accepts as data and attempts to observe and use as bases of inference. As far as can be seen now, this third division, even more than the second, is a field for the exercise of informed judgment rather than for reasoning according to the canons of science. The movements of history are to be "sensed" rather than plotted and projected into the future.

Within the compass of the first division of economics, that of economic theory, there is a practically limitless number of problems and points of view which may afford bases for separating independent variables from dependent. But we can distinguish some four or five levels in the stability of data, corresponding to stages in the causal sequence, causes at one stage becoming effects of more general and stable causes at the next. First. The price situation *at a moment* is the resultant (as far as it can be explained in terms of general forces) of a tendency to equilibrium between offers to buy and offers to sell, all of which are based upon speculative opinions. Neither the actual supplies of goods nor the ultimate demand operate *directly;* they act only indirectly in so far as the facts control the opinions of the traders, which opinions fix the prices. In highly organized markets there is a fairly effective focusing of the real speculative opinions of the persons who have any active interest in the market. In the great bulk of consumption goods there is no well-organized market, and the price at any time and place is subject to influence within rather wide limits on each side of the true competitive level by a wide variety of accidental and special factors, especially by "monopoly" in diverse forms and degrees.

Second. For most commodities there is a more or less definite production period or interval within which the supply available in the world market at least will not be much affected by price changes. As regards agricultural crops the period is sharply fixed. As regards manufactured goods it is less definite, but there is usually relative stability of supply for some period, though it may be much more quickly responsive to price changes in one direction than the other. In any case the phenomenon of a period within which supply is fairly unchangeable is general enough to justify recognition of a theory of price with reference to it. For this problem the physical quantity of supply available, or for which commitments have been made, is the supply datum, and the demand curves of the ultimate consumers are the constants on that side of the price adjustment.

Third. For longer periods of, say, a decade, the situation is more complex. The supply of any particular good is obviously a dependent variable, responsive to price forces rather than causal of them, through the shifting of productive power from one industry to another. But for such periods the total productive power of society may be treated as roughly constant (or subject to considerable change only from causes outside the regular workings of the price system). Also the population and its consumptive habits, the distribution of wealth, knowledge of technical methods, and the like may be viewed as *reasonably* independent variables. These, then, are the "causes" which control and in terms of which we explain the "dependent variables" with reference to this period, the prices of goods and of productive services and the apportionment of productive power among different industries and of product among different persons. Within such a period the extent to which productive power can actually be moved about, and at what cost, depend upon causes special to each individual situation and about which no generalization can be made.

The largest reservation called for in assuming the fixity of the data controlling production and consumption over a period of years relates to the permanence of wants. As a standard of living rises, the economic interests of people are transferred more and more out of the sphere of fundamental needs into that of aesthetic and social gratification and pure experimentation. Thus wants become more unstable and as a result the interest of producers is centered more in the field of arousing wants or changing them to fit particular products and less in the field of studying wants and producing goods to fit them. Yet although the bulk of the national expenditure now has little relation to strict physiological needs if social and aesthetic standards were to be disregarded, it is still true that most of it fits into a fairly stable set of cultural values. Only over longer periods, of generations, do the fundamental social standards and ideals change greatly. The study of such long-time changes would seem to be the most conspicuous task of institutional economics, though similar reasoning applies in a not much smaller degree to changes in the other fundamental factors of the economic situation. No one would belittle the importance of studying these historic movements in the general structure of social standards and relations which presents the fourth level stage in economic causality. But neither, we think, can anyone contend that such a study should displace the other branches of economics which either are fairly independent of institutions or take them as they are at a given time and place and use them in explaining the immediate facts of economic life.

The prospect of actually predicting the historical changes of institutions does not, as we have repeatedly observed, look very promising to us. The possibilities seem to be restricted to two main lines of approach. Institutions might be treated as entities on their own account and internal, inherent laws of growth and change found in them, which could be projected into the future. This sort of independent change, of an animistic character, is not in favor with the modern scientific mind, for the reason presumably that experience generally shows changes to be "explicable" in terms of relations to larger, more fundamental changes, in a sequence leading back to geologic and astronomical causes. This is the other alternative, to explain human culture and its movements in terms of general laws of nature and of biology, as already suggested. The work of Buckle represents perhaps the most thoroughgoing attempt yet made in this direction, and his leadership has not produced much of a school of followers. The theories of natural selection and the materialistic interpretation of history have had hard sledding and have not got far, even in explaining the past, nor anywhere in sight of the goal of power to predict. The fact seems to be that man is at heart a sentimentalist, as far, in general, as he can be and live, or at little farther. Only the animals are really "sensible," knowing what is good for them and doing it. The formula which will predict changes in the motives and conduct of men, either by discovering an internal law or by relating them in some determinate way to the predictable facts of nature, is not, we believe, likely to be discovered soon. The statements that "history repeats itself" and its equivalent, that "human nature is always the same," are true, in a sense. But it is a sense that cannot be defined, and such a sense that definite inferences drawn from the principle are more likely to be false than true. Trained judgment and human insight seem to be more effective in predicting the future than any discoverable law, and that is not going very far.

So our argument is chiefly a recital of the limitations set by the nature of the data upon the scientific treatment of human problems in general and those of an economic character in particular. In the realm of physical nature the exact methods of science have carried undertaking and control enormously further than common sense could go. But this was because the data are relatively stable, reducible to classes of manageable number, and especially classes with recognizable and measurable indices. None of these essential features seem to hold good of human data. Moreover, in any deep view of the case, the problem of understanding and controlling human behavior is radically different in character from that of explaining the material world and using it. Physical objects are not at the same time trying to understand and use the investigator! The practical problem of getting along with our fellow human beings must be attacked in the main by a method very different from the technique of natural science, a different kind of development and refinement of common sense, which carries us rather into the fields of aesthetics. In a limited field in economic data, due largely to the fact that exchange has reduced the factors to definite measurable quantities, we can have an exact science of the general form of relations. It can tell us little in the concrete, and its chief function is negative — to offset as far as possible the stupid theorizing of the man in the street. The real sociology and economics must be branches of literature as much as of science. In fact they need to be both, and commonly succeed in being neither. It is no wonder that these sciences are still in the stage of violent disagreement among their followers as to what they are and what they are about. The first step toward getting out of this slough, we suggest, is to recognize that man's relations with his fellow men are on a totally different footing from his relations with the objects of physical nature and to give up, except within recognized and rather narrow limits, the naive project of carrying over a technique which has been successful in the one set of problems and using it to solve another set of a categorically different kind.

Notes

1. The "new" logic of modern mathematics and neo-realist philosophy, dealing with empty relations and pure order, if it has any relation to conduct at all, has so little that it can be left out of account in such a survey as the present.

2. The argument of earlier sections of the essay should have made it clear that only within restricted limits are wants to be regarded as data for science in any case. Civilized people act perhaps as much by way of experimentation in wants and satisfaction as they do in response to wants for definite things. But explorative behavior cannot be rationally directed in the sense in which action directed toward a foreseen result is rational, and it is apparently without the pale of strictly scientific treatment.

BIBLIOGRAPHY

Becker, Gary S. *The Economic Approach to Human Behavior*. Chicago: University of Chicago Press, 1976.

———. *Economic Theory*. New York: Alfred Knopf, 1971.

Boulding, Kenneth E. "Economics as a Moral Science." *Economics as a Science*. New York: McGraw-Hill, 1970.

———. *Economics as a Science*. New York: McGraw-Hill, 1970.

Brennan, Geoffrey, and James Buchanan. "The Normative Purpose of Economic 'Science': Rediscovery of an Eighteenth Century Method." Liberty Fund Conference, "Science, Markets, and Individual Freedom," San Antonio, Texas, March 1981.

Buchanan, James M. *The Reason for Rules*. Cambridge: Cambridge University Press, forthcoming.

———. *The Limits of Liberty: Between Anarchy and Leviathan*. Chicago: University of Chicago Press, 1975.

———. "Is Economics a Science of Choice?" In *Roads to Freedom: Essays in Honor of Friedrich A. Hayek,* Erich Streissler, ed., London: Routledge and Kegan Paul, 1969.

———. "Reflection on the Alchian Method of Economic Analysis." Unpublished draft. Blacksburg: Center for the Study of Public Choice, Virginia Polytechnic Institute and State University, 1969.

Coddington, Allen. "Positive Economics." *Canadian Journal of Economics,* February 1972.

"Degrees of Evaluation." *The Ethics of Competition and Other Essays*. New York: Harper and Brothers, 1935.

Dolan, Edwin G. "Austrian Economics as Extraordinary Science." *The Foundations of Modern Austrian Economics*. Kansas City, Mo.: Sheed and Ward, 1976.

———, ed. *The Foundations of Modern Austrian Economics*. Menlo Park, Calif.: Institute for Human Studies, 1976.

119

Friedman, Milton. "The Methodology of Positive Economics." *Essays in Positive Economics*. Chicago: University of Chicago Press, 1953.

Hayek, Friedrich A. *Law, Legislation, and Liberty*. 3 volumes. Chicago: University of Chicago Press, 1973, 1976, and 1979.

———. *New Studies in Philosophy, Politics, Economics, and the History of Ideas*. Chicago: University of Chicago Press, 1978.

———. "Degrees of Explanation: The Theory of Complex Phenomena." *Studies in Philosophy, Politics, and Economics*. Chicago: University of Chicago Press, 1967.

———. "The Economy, Science, and Politics." *Studies in Philosophy, Politics and Economics*. Chicago: University of Chicago Press, 1967.

———. "Economics and Knowledge." *Individualism and Economic Order*. Chicago: University of Chicago Press, 1948.

———. "The Facts of the Social Sciences." *Individualism and Economic Order*. Chicago: University of Chicago Press, 1948.

———. "Scientism and the Study of Society." *The Counter-Revolution of Science*. Chicago: University of Chicago Press, 1952.

———. *The Road to Serfdom*. Chicago: University of Chicago Press, 1942.

Heath, Anthony. *Rational Choice and Social Exchange: A Critique of Exchange Theory*. Cambridge: University Press, 1976.

Heyne, Paul. *The Economic Way of Thinking*. 2d ed. Chicago: Science Research Associates, 1976.

———. "The Use and Abuse of the Normative-Positive Distinction." Southern Economic Association Annual Meeting, November 1974.

Kagel, John H., Raymond C. Batallio, Howard Kachlin, and Leonard Green. "Demand Curves for Animal Consumers." *Quarterly Journal of Economics*, February 1981.

Kirzner, Israel M. *Competition and Entrepreneurship*. Chicago: University of Chicago Press, 1973.

———. "On the Method of Austrian Economics." In *The Foundations of Modern Austrian Economics*, Edwin G. Dolan, ed., Menlo Park, Calif.: Institute for Human Studies, 1976.

Knight, Frank H. "Fact and Values in Social Science." *Freedom and Reform: Essays in Economics and Social Philosophy*. Port Washington, N.Y.: Kennikat Press, 1969.

———. "The Planful Act: The Possibilities and Limitations of Collective Rationality." *Freedom and Reform: Essays in Economics and Social Philosophy*.

———. *Risk, Uncertainty, and Profit*. New York: Augustus M. Kelly, 1921 and 1951.

———. *Freedom and Reform: Essays in Economics and Social Philosophy*. New York: Harper, 1947.

———. "The Limitations of Scientific Method in Economics." *The Ethics of Competition*. Chicago: University of Chicago Press, 1936.

Loasby, Brian J. *Choice, Complexity, and Ignorance*. Cambridge: Cambridge University Press, 1976.

Machan, Tibor. "The Non-Rational Domain and the Limits of Economics: Comments." *Southern Economic Journal*, April 1981.

McKenzie, Richard B., and Gordon Tullock. *The New World of Economics: Explorations into Human Experience*. Homewood, Ill.: Richard D. Irwin, 1975, 1978, and 1981.

McKinney, John. "Frank H. Knight on Uncertainty and Reactional Action." *Southern Economic Journal*, April 1977.

Marshall, Alfred. "The Present Position of Economics." *Memorial of Alfred Marshall,* A.C. Pigou, ed. London: Macmillan and Company, 1925.

Mises, Ludwig von. *Human Action: A Treatise on Economics.* New Haven, Ct.: Yale University Press, 1949, 1963.

———. *The Ultimate Foundation of Economics.* Kansas City, M.: Andrews and McNeel, 1962.

Mundel, Robert A. *Man and Economics.* New York: McGraw-Hill, 1968.

Nozick, Robert. *Anarchy, State, and Utopia.* New York: Basic Books, 1974.

Officer, Lawrence H., and Leana Stiefel. "The New World of Economics: A Review Article." *Journal of Economic Issues* 10 (March 1976).

Rawls, John. *A Theory of Justice.* Cambridge, Mass.: Harvard University Press, 1971.

Robbins, Lionel. *The Nature and Significance of Economic Science.* 2d ed. Macmillan 1973.

Rothbard, Murry H. *Individualism and the Philosophy of the Social Sciences.* San Francisco: Cato Institute, 1979.

———. "Praxeology: The Methodology of Austrian Economics." In *The Foundations of Modern Austrian Economics,* Edwin G. Dolan, ed. Kansas City, Mo.: Sheed and Ward, 1976.

Samuels, Warren J. "The Necessary Normative Context of Positive Economics: Comment." *Journal of Economic Issues* 15 (September 1981): 721–27.

———. "Economics as a Science and Its Relation to Policy: The Example of Free Trade." *Journal of Economic Issues* 14 (March 1980): 163–85.

———. ed. *The Chicago School of Political Economy.* East Lansing: University of Michigan Press, 1977.

Samuelson, Paul. "Problems of Methodology: Discussion." *American Economic Review,* May 1963.

Schoeck, Helmut, and James W. Wiggins, eds. "Introduction." *Scientism and Values.* Princeton, N.J.: D. Van Nostrand, 1960.

———, eds. *Scientism and Values.* New York: D. Van Nostrand, 1960.

Stigler, George. *Lecture I, II, and III.* Harvard University, Cambridge, Mass., April 1980.

———. *The Citizen and the State: Essays on Regulation.* Chicago: University of Chicago Press, 1975.

———. "The Economist and the State." *The Citizen and the State: Essays on Regulation.* Chicago: University of Chicago Press, 1975.

———. "The Politics of Political Economists." *Quarterly Journal of Economics* 73 (November 1959).

Stigler, George, and Gary S. Becker. "De Gustibus Non Est Disputandum." *American Economic Review,* March 1977.

Stressler, Erich, ed. *Roads to Freedom.* London: Routledge and Kegan Paul, 1969.

Tenascio, Vincent J. *Pareto's Methodological Approach to Economics.* Chapel Hill: University of North Carolina Press, 1968.

Watts, Michael. "The Non-Rational Domain and the Limits of Economics: Comments." *Southern Economic Journal,* April 1981.

Wicksteed, Philip H. *The Common Sense Political Economy.* New York: Augustus M. Kelly, 1967.

Index